MW01113792

Praise for *Inside the Minds*

"What C-Level executives read to keep their edge and make pivotal business decisions. Timeless classics for indispensable knowledge." - Richard Costello, Manager of Corporate Marketing Communication, General Electric

"Want to know what the real leaders are thinking about now? It's in here." - Carl Ledbetter, SVP & CTO, Novell, Inc.

"Priceless wisdom from experts at applying technology in support of business objectives." - Frank Campagnoni, CTO, GE Global Exchange Services

"Unique insights into the way the experts think and the lessons they've learned from experience." - MT Rainey, Co-CEO, Young & Rubicam/Rainey Kelly Campbell Roalfe

"A must-read for anyone in the industry." - Dr. Chuck Lucier, Chief Growth Officer, Booz-Allen & Hamilton

"Unlike any other business books, *Inside the Minds* captures the essence, the deep-down thinking processes, of people who make things happen." - Martin Cooper, CEO, Arraycomm

"A must-read for those who manage at the intersection of business and technology." - Frank Roney, General Manager, IBM

"A great way to see across the changing marketing landscape at a time of significant innovation." - David Kenny, Chairman & CEO, Digitas

"An incredible resource of information to help you develop outside the box..." - Rich Jernstedt, CEO, Golin/Harris International

"A snapshot of everything you need to know..." - Larry Weber, Founder, Weber Shandwick

"Great information for both novices and experts." - Patrick Ennis, Partner, ARCH Venture Partners

"The only useful way to get so many good minds speaking on a complex topic." - Scott Bradner, Senior Technical Consultant, Harvard University

"Must-have information for business executives." - Alex Wilmerding, Principal, Boston Capital Ventures

www.Aspatore.com

Aspatore Books is the largest and most exclusive publisher of C-Level executives (CEO, CFO, CTO, CMO, Partner) from the world's most respected companies and law firms. Aspatore annually publishes a select group of C-Level executives from the Global 1,000, top 250 law firms (partners and chairs), and other leading companies of all sizes. C-Level Business Intelligence™, as conceptualized and developed by Aspatore Books, provides professionals of all levels with proven business intelligence from industry insiders – direct and unfiltered insight from those who know it best – as opposed to third-party accounts offered by unknown authors and analysts. Aspatore Books is committed to publishing an innovative line of business and legal books, those which lay forth principles and offer insights that when employed, can have a direct financial impact on the reader's business objectives, whatever they may be. In essence, Aspatore publishes critical tools – need-to-read as opposed to nice-to-read books – for all business professionals.

Inside the Minds

The critically acclaimed *Inside the Minds* series provides readers of all levels with proven business intelligence from C-Level executives (CEO, CFO, CTO, CMO, partner) from the world's most respected companies. Each chapter is comparable to a white paper or essay and is a future-oriented look at where an industry/profession/topic is heading and the most important issues for future success. Each author has been carefully chosen through an exhaustive selection process by the *Inside the Minds* editorial board to write a chapter for this book. *Inside the Minds* was conceived in order to give readers actual insights into the leading minds of business executives worldwide. Because so few books or other publications are actually written by executives in industry, *Inside the Minds* presents an unprecedented look at various industries and professions never before available.

CFO Leadership Strategies

Industry Leaders on Financial Integrity, Compliance, and Best Practices

BOOK IDEA SUBMISSIONS

If you are a C-Level executive or senior lawyer interested in submitting a book idea or manuscript to the Aspatore editorial board, please e-mail authors@aspatore.com. Aspatore is especially looking for highly specific book ideas that would have a direct financial impact on behalf of a reader. Completed books can range from 20 to 2,000 pages – the topic and "need to read" aspect of the material are most important, not the length. Include your book idea, biography, and any additional pertinent information.

SPEAKER SUBMISSIONS FOR CONFERENCES

If you are interested at giving a speech for an upcoming ReedLogic conference (a partner of Aspatore Books), please e-mail the ReedLogic Speaker Board at speakers@reedlogic.com. If selected, speeches are given over the phone and recorded (no travel necessary). Due to the busy schedules and travel implications for executives, ReedLogic produces each conference on CD-ROM, then distributes the conference to bookstores and executives who register for the conference. The finished CD-ROM includes the speaker picture with the audio of the speech playing in the background, similar to a radio address played on television.

INTERACTIVE SOFTWARE SUBMISSIONS

If you have an idea for an interactive business or software legal program, please e-mail software@reedlogic.com. ReedLogic is especially looking for Excel spreadsheet models and PowerPoint presentations that help business professionals and lawyers achieve specific tasks. If idea or program is accepted, product is distributed to bookstores nationwide.

Published by Aspatore, Inc.

For corrections, company/title updates, comments or any other inquiries please e-mail store@aspatore.com.

First Printing, 2005
10 9 8 7 6 5 4 3 2 1

ISBN 1-59622-264-6
Library of Congress Control Number: 2005931051

Inside the Minds Managing Editor, Laura Kearns, Edited by Eddie Fournier, Proofread by Brian Denitzio

Material in this book is for educational purposes only. This book is sold with the understanding that neither any of the authors or the publisher is engaged in rendering legal, accounting, investment, or any other professional service. Neither the publisher nor the authors assume any liability for any errors or omissions or for how this book or its contents are used or interpreted or for any consequences resulting directly or indirectly from the use of this book. For legal advice or any other, please consult your personal lawyer or the appropriate professional.

The views expressed by the individuals in this book (or the individuals on the cover) do not necessarily reflect the views shared by the companies they are employed by (or the companies mentioned in this book). The employment status and affiliations of authors with the companies referenced are subject to change.

CFO Leadership Strategies

Industry Leaders on Financial Integrity, Compliance, and Best Practices

Contents

Financial Integrity and Compliance Success

James W. Noyce

Chief Financial Officer

FBL Financial Group, Inc.

Goals of My Position

My key responsibility is ensuring the financial integrity of the company, in overseeing all financial aspects of the organization, including the accounting department, as well as areas of investment and information technology. I am expected to ensure that all financial aspects of the organization are taken care of, and a strong aspect of that responsibility lies in compliance.

Why is compliance such a strong factor? We're in a highly regulated industry, so we're dealing with a lot of compliance issues other industries don't necessarily deal with. We're also a public company. Many of the compliance issues regarding Sarbanes-Oxley and all of the Securities and Exchange Commission (SEC) and New York Stock Exchange requirements are also relevant to my company. Insurance actually has its own brand of accounting that is different than that of other industries. Even the financial statement, the look of the balance sheet, and the operating statement are unique to insurance companies.

As a member of the senior management team, I feel it's important for me to keep other members of senior management informed about financial and compliance issues we as a company must address.

My second significant contribution is taking on the role of expense czar, in having oversight of the part of our organization that probably spends the most time on expense control aspects.

Expense Control Vigilance

While my role is of a kind of czar, our organization also has the mechanism where we have set up a committee with oversight of expense control. The person who chairs that committee is our vice president of finance, who reports to me.

I am also involved in capital management, in looking at our business from segment and product standpoints to understand where we're making money, and to distribute that information to various department heads to help us make sure we're allocating our capital in the most meaningful way.

Keys to CFO Success

Today's chief financial officer (CFO) needs technical skills to understand the financial aspects of the organization. Regarding the role of CFO for an insurance company, one needs to know the issues insurance companies have to deal with regarding such activities as accounting and financial reporting. Equally as important, the CFO must have the communication skills, both written and verbal, in order to relay what's going on within the financial side of the business.

Communication skills cannot be underestimated. Beyond the books and accounting, a CFO needs to communicate important information clearly to the rest of senior management, to the board of directors, and to outside constituents—shareholders, regulators, and rating agencies.

At the top of the list rests a high level of integrity and willingness to pound the table with regards to preserving integrity: The successful CFO makes sure things are not just done well, but that they are done in the right way and appropriately.

Compliance and Personal Integrity

I serve as the chief compliance officer of the organization, which means chairing a lot of our various committees. One of the things people need to do in those positions is to make sure they are demonstrating high levels of honesty and integrity in the workplace and in their personal life. It all comes down to leadership by example.

If you just pound the table and talk about those things, but don't actually demonstrate them, I don't think you get follow-through from the rest of the employee base.

Risk Assessment

Any CFO needs to have a very good understanding of risks that face the business, unique either to that person's company or industry. That would apply to all organizations, and I think the CFO needs to be especially vigilant in understanding the financial implications. One success strategy is to make sure you have a firm grasp of all the risks associated with your business and how you are going to eliminate, manage, or mitigate those elements of risk.

Prioritizing the Challenges: A First Step

Each day brings new challenges. Perhaps the central challenge is accepting the fact that no two days are the same. What stays the same is that one can always expect to have to deal with complicated issues. When a problem lands on my desk, it's often because some other very bright people are having a difficult time dealing with it. You couple that with the burden of financial oversight of different aspects of the organization, and the amount of time this oversight consumes.

What one must do is establish priorities on where to best utilize time. It is a matter of balancing the specific, complex issues, but at the same time carrying forward an overall strategy and direction of the business.

Paying Attention to Working Relationships

I work closely with the very top, the entire board of directors. I have a close working relationship with them, especially the members of the audit committee, because I am the primary contact for them.

The chief executive officer (CEO) and I spend a great deal of time together. He relies on me as a sounding board, certainly for all the financial aspects of the organization, but also for many operational strategies as well.

I work with all three division heads. One heads up our primary life distribution, another heads our primary property casualty distribution, and another heads our alternative distribution for life and annuity products.

Then there are other members of our senior management that actually report to me. They include the vice president of finance for all the financial and accounting aspects of the organization, our chief technology officer, and our chief investment officer.

The important requirement governing all these relationships is to acquire a rapport and understanding, in addition to a level of trust within an organization's senior management. One needs to know how to deal with each as an individual and then how to deal with them as a team. What are their risk appetites? What are their risk tolerances?

Also, beyond numbers, a CFO must understand what's happening in their marketplace. Questions to ask: What are our levels of operational expertise? Where do we have core competencies? Where within the organization should we look for outsourcing opportunities?

It's quite helpful if the CFO understands the marketplace the company is trying to sell into through its various divisions. As a CFO, you need to understand those things in order to really know what the opportunities are.

Building a Team

When building a team, I look for the same qualities that must be present in the CFO. By this I mean the team members need the technical skills necessary for their part of the organization. For the finance and accounting areas they need to have expertise in statutory and GAAP insurance accounting, SEC rules and regulations, how to do investigative analysis of financial accounting statements, and the like.

They need to show knowledge of tax-related issues where necessary from both the investment and technology side. They need the technical skills required to understand the discipline in which they're involved.

The next quality I look for is honesty and integrity. I want to see them wearing those qualities on their lapels.

I want people that are willing to come in and tell me what they believe, even if they think it might not necessarily be what I want to hear. I like people that can be totally honest and get the issues on the table without emotion, and then deal with them in an objective fashion.

Next, I want to see evidence of the strong communication skills I mentioned earlier. The people working with me most closely are typically going to have fairly large departments reporting to them. They need to have the skills to communicate their expectations to their people, and to communicate up the chain of command to myself and other members of senior management. They will need to articulate what the issues are and how they're being dealt with.

Fundamentally, we want to develop new leadership here as we move forward. I think we're interested in people that are looking at being lifelong learners—learning new methods of management and leadership, and interested in developing their leadership skills. This has worked well for us, and we continue to internally generate strong leadership in our organization.

Setting Annual Goals

We establish our goals within our organization on a very global basis. We have a set of corporate goals every year by which everybody is measured. Our annual incentive bonus program, in which every employee participates at various levels, is tied directly to those goals.

We have specific numeric goals that fall into the areas of growth measured by production and growth in number of customers. We have efficiency goals that we measure through expense control, and we have profitability goals measured for our public company by earnings per share. For our property casualty company, profitability is based on a combined ratio basis, which measures the underwriting profitability of the organization.

We publish the goals monthly, so everybody within the organization knows where we stand with regard to those goals. We are compensated once a year through a bonus program based on those goals.

Now, with regard to goals that are not necessarily numeric or quantitative in nature, but more qualitative and subjective, there is an annual review process where I sit down with each member of the team and go through the achievements the person has had in the past year. We discuss expectations, and we set specific goals for that individual.

These might be in the form of education, development of their staff, overall performance measures, and things like that. My style is to have regular discussions with each member of the team regarding how they're doing, so there are no real surprises at the annual review.

I'm a firm believer that you need to look for ways to compliment people and not just tear them down in order to get the highest performance levels possible.

Cost Areas

Benchmarking preparedness for Sarbanes-Oxley is the law—as a public company, we really have no choice. Any company that does not get the work done could experience significant impact in the way the marketplace views them and, therefore, their share price could be affected.

Within our organization, elements of Sarbanes-Oxley led to some changes to the structure of our board of directors in order to meet some of the governance requirements. We have more committee meetings than we had before. Charters for some of our committees had to be drafted and published. Those things have cost some money and certainly some time.

From an economic and cost standpoint, I'd say those have not been as significant as the compliance with Section 404 of Sarbanes-Oxley. That has to do with the documentation and testing of our internal control environment. We are essentially going to pay our auditing firm twice as much this year as we have paid them in the past, which is directly related to their certification of SOX 404.

In addition, we have utilized a consulting firm to help ensure that we are going about 404 compliance in an appropriate way, and we have spent significant money for those services. Our internal audit department of five people spent essentially all of their time working on 404 activities for the past year, and many department heads spent significant time with documentation and testing.

We estimate that the total cost of 404 compliance this first year is going to be somewhere between $2 million and $3 million, which for a company our size is a significant amount.

Preparedness Advice

The CEO needs to set a direction at the top. The CEO needs to communicate that the company needs to be in compliance with all aspects of the Sarbanes-Oxley 404 and make it a priority to obtain that objective.

Next, it is the responsibility of the CEO and the CFO to address certifications every quarter. The way we do that is by meeting with all of the division heads and going through the requirements of that certification process, making sure everyone is in agreement that we have in fact complied with all of those. Each of the division heads has a responsibility to make sure their unit is also in compliance with the elements of Sarbanes-Oxley. It is each division head's responsibility to oversee that, to review that documentation process for completeness and accuracy, and ultimately to sign off on it.

There will be a lot of companies that are going to have material weaknesses and are not going to get a clean opinion with regards to 404. In my view, that doesn't necessarily mean they haven't reached the minimal level. It could mean they've done everything they can. But these requirements are so new and so complex, some companies may not find it possible to make all the changes necessary.

I think companies will need, within the next year, to get to a position where they have mediated their material weaknesses. We're coming close to the end of the year. This is the first time we're going to have to comply with all 404 activities.

Trigger Points and Spending

The magnitude of the material weaknesses will dictate what the shareholder reaction to that level of non-compliance will be. The most significant trigger point is being in compliance to a level that the internal auditors can give us a clean opinion. Our goal and objective is:

1. to make sure there's no material weaknesses within our internal control structure, and
2. to make sure any significant deficiencies are identified and dealt with as expediently as possible.

With regards to SOX 404, there is no way to reduce the cost. Frankly, requirements dictate that the external auditors come in to review all the documentation, test controls and processes, and ultimately sign off on them. Our auditing firm is working as efficiently as possible, but it's all new. Therefore, money is being spent on the external auditors, and in our case we spent some money on consulting to help us develop our systems of documentation and testing.

One can argue that it's money we could have avoided spending, but I believe that we needed to spend it. I think it was appropriate, because we've never been through it before, and it was worth having some outside expertise to guide us through the process.

The department heads have mainly been involved in the documentation and working with internal and external auditors on the testing. Those things all have to happen for this project to be successful, and they're going to have to happen every year. I don't think there's great opportunity for improvement on spending.

In the meantime, we have learned something about our internal control structure that may lead to a few better methods of internal control. For the most part, however, there's been very little benefit from the expenditure of this money.

Payback in Vigilance

From my perspective, the most important aspects of Sarbanes-Oxley are the governance and oversight of the organization.

- It's making sure senior management is setting the right tone at the top.
- It's making sure the board of directors is paying attention to the strategies and risks of the organization.

- It's making sure appropriate risk-related decisions are being made.
- It's keeping an eye on management and asking the difficult questions of management to make sure things are being done in an appropriate fashion.

I think the intent of the Sarbanes-Oxley Act was to legislate that those things happen. In my mind, at FBL, that's what we were doing before, and now after, Sarbanes-Oxley. Because we believe that's the way organizations are supposed to operate.

If the boards of directors are doing their job, and keeping an eye on the ball and asking the difficult questions, and if audit committees are really digging in, then those types of unfortunate incidents that occurred at certain companies in the past can be avoided in the future.

Reducing Spending

Self-Imposed Target Levels

We have reduced our corporate spending in the last few years, and it might be helpful to discuss our organizational approach toward expense control.

Very senior levels of management serve on our Expense Control Task Force. It includes myself and the heads of the various departments and divisions, such as the chief marketing officer and the chief technology officer. We established a methodology a few years ago of benchmarking our expenses. We use an outside service that comes every year, reviews the trends we have, and benchmarks us against other peer groups and companies.

As a result, we've given ourselves some overall target levels of expenses, and those aren't necessarily specific dollar thresholds. They are more ratios with regards to revenues, so we can run on somewhat of a variable cost structure. We know if we grow faster, there are certain elements of our business where we will have to spend more money. That is suitable, as long as the ratios stay within the targets we have set.

Two of our goals every year are specifically tied to expense budgets we established. We actually go through a very rigorous budget process, where this expense task force establishes goals. The benchmarking process serves to really break things down into very specific areas.

As a result, we can see where we need to target in order to reach a best practices level with our expenditures. We've made significant progress in this regard. We have also been through several mergers in the past few years. Consolidation that ensued really allowed us to target some areas and make specific headway with expenditure levels.

All in all, expense control is a never-ending job. As soon as you take your eye off that ball, certain business elements start to get a little out of hand in regard to spending levels. Someone needs to keep an eye on that regularly. We do expense budget variance reports every quarter. As explained previously, we establish targets annually after we've been through the benchmarking process.

The Challenge of Information Technology

In confronting challenges, information technology is a difficult one to address, because the return on investment is quite elusive. It seems as if we are spending more and more on technology all the time in the quest to do things more efficiently. Technology is changing so fast that there is a strong urge to keep moving with the newest and greatest technological advances.

In my observation, looking for those technology opportunities might mean you will spend more money in the short term, but, if they work, will generate a big savings once fully implemented.

A clear example of that is our experience right now in a conversion of some legacy systems for policyholder processing on the property side of our business to a new package policy. We have spent millions of dollars on this new system.

We're in the process of converting to that new system right now, and we are kind of double spending as a result. But when we are converted, we'll be able to turn off that series of legacy systems and save many millions of dollars over what we've spent on this new system. So, technology can represent opportunity. The pattern is usually an investment followed by savings.

As CFO, one must be extremely disciplined. It is easy to head down a technology path where you don't end up getting the savings you expected. So, one must watch spending on technology, especially the new bells and whistles. I think this is the area where some companies may tend to let spending get out of hand.

As a result, information technology represents a challenging area that is not as simple and straightforward as other areas to be addressed. Once you've spent the money, it's difficult to rein the spending back in. Once technology is deployed, you must support it.

How does one avoid making such costly errors in information technology? The way we do it here is to make sure any changes in the deployment of technology are brought to our management team, discussed, and approved at that level. It is necessary to consider the expected deliverables, such as improved customer service, or just plain cost savings. Otherwise, people are going to tend to want to get the latest and greatest technological advances. I believe it is up to senior management to exercise the discipline required.

A Handle on Health Costs

Certainly, healthcare costs affect a company's bottom line. Healthcare costs have been one of the highest items as far as a percentage increase, and costs have escalated over several years.

A few years ago, we went to a self-funding program. We went from a fully insured plan to essentially a self-insured plan, and we're paying a health insurance company to administer the benefits of that plan. That helped us move forward pretty dramatically. It's amazing how much money we saved: $2 million, $3 million dollars a year in savings just from that move alone.

In moving forward, we have done some things to make it more evident to employees how much healthcare really costs. We've done this through increased deductibles. We compare what we are charging our employees as opposed to the premium the health insurance really costs. We then show them their savings. This has made our employees more aware of the true cost, and we think that's helped control costs as well.

We also note the presence of generic drugs versus name brand drugs by being willing to pay more of the cost of the generic drugs, as they are significantly less expensive. What's more, we have just increased the levels of deductibles for employees. We go through a flexible spending program, so there's a little more cost sharing by the employee group.

Outsourcing vs. Offshoring

We've done nothing offshore. We have looked at opportunities there, mostly with programming and information technology applications, but we have not done that yet. I think our view at this point is that we may not be a big enough organization to really take advantage of offshore opportunities.

Outsourcing is a different story. We do outsource certain elements of our business that we do not believe involve our core competencies, and we continually explore others. For example, the large outgoing mail jobs that require print have been outsourced to an organization that has expertise in that area. We give them information and they do the printing, the stuffing, the postage, and the mailing. We take advantage of some pretty significant savings as a result. So far, it's all been done with local or regional vendors.

On the other hand, there are areas we would never consider outsourcing, as they are within our core competencies, such as the claims handling of our property casualty claims or investment management, where we have approximately $10 billion of investments under management.

Steps for Action

In recommending cost-cutting steps for other organizations, I think first you have to appoint a group of people who have the required knowledge and are senior enough to be effective in making it happen. The team's objective should be expense cutting.

Next, you need to set some objectives and some goals, both short-term and long-term, as to where you want to get from an expenditure-level standpoint. Then you have to be disciplined towards reaching those goals.

We helped ourselves establish those goals through the benchmarking process I described. I'm sure there are other tools that would be available to help establish and set your goals, but I think having some view of what typical expenditure levels are within your industry and your peer group is important, to make sure you're on the right track.

James W. Noyce is the chief financial officer for FBL Financial Group, Inc. of West Des Moines, Iowa, a group of companies offering life insurance and investment products to members/clients throughout the United States through exclusive and independent agents, and property/casualty products in eight states through exclusive agents.

Mr. Noyce joined the companies in 1985. He has held various positions, including financial planning manager, financial planning vice president, controller, and executive vice president and general manager of the property/casualty division. He was promoted to the position of CFO in 1995.

Mr. Noyce is a fellow of the Casualty Actuarial Society, a member of the American Academy of Actuaries, an associate of the Society of Actuaries, a certified public accountant, and a fellow of the Life Management Institute. He is involved in many civic and industry organizations, including board member of the Special Olympics Iowa and the Mid-Iowa Council of Boy Scouts of America, member of the board of trustees of Grand View College, president of Des Moines Golf and Country Club, past chairman of Junior Achievement of Central Iowa, past president of the West Des Moines Rotary Club, youth softball and roller hockey coach, past member of the executive committee of the NAII Tax Committee, member of the advisory committee of the American Agricultural Insurance Company, and member of the advisory committee of the Farm Bureau Bank.

Mr. Noyce and his wife, Shelley, reside in West Des Moines and have three children.

Dedication: *To Kathleen Till Stange.*

Preparing for Financial Risks

Robert J. Dellinger

Executive Vice President and Chief Financial Officer

Sprint Corporation

The Role of a CFO

As CFO, I'm trying to ensure we have a bulletproof company, and that means bulletproof from a standpoint of financial preparedness, governance preparedness, and business risk preparedness. So if something should change dramatically, we'll be well positioned to survive it; it's a long-term viability view. I want to ensure that we are driving flexibility in the ability to change, because I believe, for most companies, that the one trait that may make them unique and truly competitive is their ability to adapt and change quickly.

It's hard in this industry, or most industries for that matter, to say, "Oh, we're always going to be the most innovative, or we're going to have the best network, or the highest quality product." Well, others can duplicate those assets. They can hire some engineers and they can recreate that fairly easily in many cases. Or they can lower the price and be the price leader. Your ability to adapt and change based on your environment, I think, is a truly unique competitive advantage, and one you get to maintain for the long term. And that's very hard to duplicate.

Finally, a clear goal is creating shareholder value for the short and long term, which is best measured by stock price improvement. Is our entity worth more a year from now than it is worth today?

I work hard at driving change, making sure we have a culture and an organization that is flexible, and knows how to adapt to change. That's something I believe in very strongly, and it's always one of my key messages when I'm meeting with employees.

I take very strong positions. Sometimes, I am a voice of dissent in business debates, because I think we need to challenge our thinking and take different positions. I defend my views as best I can with facts. But even if the facts don't support it, I'll sometimes sit on the other side of the issue to encourage thinking. I'm always focused on optimizing our financial structure and making sure it's stronger than it was the period before, the quarter before, or the year before.

Successful CFOs

As a chief financial officer, I think you have to have presence, because you spend a lot of time in front of other business leaders, customers, employees, and shareholders. But you also need to have some passion for the job, because it's not always the most fun job. Trust me, there are many more entertaining jobs, and I've had a few of them. It is critical to have passion for your position—it drives the company forward.

Then you have to have breadth and balance. I think you need breadth, because you do have to play across the entire organization, and you have to know a little about a lot. You're not likely to be super deep in any one discipline. You're in a marketing conversation or a network conversation or a new product launch or pricing, and you have to be able to play pretty broadly across those disciplines.

I think you have to have balance, because you have to recognize business is very much about tradeoffs. There are very few optimal decisions, where something is absolutely the right thing to do. There are always tradeoffs. For example, you may spend a little more money in a certain area than perhaps you should, because there's a larger upside or it will help something else.

The Unique Telecommunications Industry

In our industry, there is a great deal of complexity with a mix of unregulated and highly regulated industries. We have a high tax environment. Telecommunications is among the highest taxed products in the United States. It's unique from that perspective.

The other thing to note is this is a business of scale. You have to be big to be successful, and scale businesses tend to get confused about pricing. They get into incremental pricing. That's clearly an issue in telecommunications, just like it is in the airline industry.

For example, in telecommunications we may build a big pipe that goes underground and can haul large chunks of data traffic. There's a tendency to think that because it's not full, shouldn't we lower prices to fill up the last

10 or 20 percent of that pipe? Well, the reality is, as you do that, you start driving price reductions on the first minute on the pipe. The airlines have clearly gone through this and have seen it. As they lowered prices on the last couple seats on the plane, it drove a reduction in the price of first class and actually created new discount competitors like Southwest Airlines and Jet Blue. So scale and incremental pricing would probably be two key challenges in the telecommunications industry.

CFO Challenges

I believe some of the most challenging aspects are the breadth and the scope, and I think you do that with time and experience and a willingness to default to your intuition when you have a lack of facts or hands-on experience. I believe that during your business career, most successful people develop very good intuition skills, and they know what's right and what's wrong without having a big twenty-page briefing book. I think your ability to do that in this role is very important.

Another very challenging aspect is multiple constituencies. You have the board, the chief executive officer, and the chief operations officer (COO), and then the shareholders. You also have senior management, debt holders, and employees, and they all want something a little bit different. Your ability to balance across that whole range of constituencies and give something to everybody is critically important to your success.

Working with the Team

I work regularly with the CEO and the COO, consumer and business division leaders, information technology and network, which are the key functions, and to a lesser degree, human resources and public relations. I spend a lot of time with our investor relations team because of our need to communicate regularly with investors. And whenever we make an announcement, we want to know what the implications are from the investors' perspective.

Unlike the CFO role, the CEO role is more challenging, because you have to balance more among employees, customers, and shareholders. The CFO should be leaning harder toward shareholders. I think you have to recognize that difference.

So as CFO, you may go to your CEO or to the board and say, "This is the right thing from the shareholder's perspective," and they may say, "Well, what about our employees or our customers?" And you just have to recognize that it's their job to rebalance those decisions. I think if you put yourself in their chair for an hour, you realize that's exactly what they have to do, and that's their job. Their job descriptions are slightly broader.

When it comes to a member of my team, I'm looking for leadership skills, communication skills, the ability to set a vision for their part of the organization, and the raw talent to drive execution. I'm less concerned about whether they're the world's best accountant or the world's best number cruncher. I'm more concerned about those broader skills. At that level of leadership, they need those broader skills.

We certainly have some formal metrics and formal scorecards in place to monitor those things, but I do a lot more of it by walking around. I have a weekly meeting with all my direct reports individually, one on one. We have a staff meeting usually every other week, but a lot more of it is accomplished by office visits or phone calls. I'm not sure my direct reports like it, but I feel very comfortable and very free to call anybody who works for them, and I do that quite regularly.

You don't do that to disrupt the management chain, but you do it to save time and get direct to the source. It also communicates to those people that you're wide open for them to call you, and I think that's important. I'm not looking for a director, who might report to my leadership team, to be all-knowledgeable about everything that's going on in their organization. I'd rather have them working on the right issues and driving the right kind of change and having people below them that they trust to get the job done.

Golden Rules

Expect the unexpected, and plan and prepare for it. So if you think, "Oh, that's the absolute worst case," well, plan for that one, and if something better happens, that'll be good news.

Lead in driving change, work to create a more flexible organization, and put your stamp on the organization—it has to reflect you. If it doesn't, I don't think you've made your presence felt.

Be visible and outspoken. As a leader of a large organization, they expect you to take positions and make some tough calls, and they don't know what happens in all these meetings, or what happens in the boardroom when the doors close. But they have to trust that when an issue comes up, you're a voice for their position. I think when they see you do that, they appreciate it.

Cost Reductions

I believe benchmarking is a very effective way to enable cost reductions, because if there's somebody else who's doing it better than you are, it's pretty hard to say, "Well, that's not real."

Yes, you can hire people who can help you with it, but you can also get a fair amount of public data. There's a fair amount of competitive intelligence that surfaces, and there are even industry organizations that accumulate this stuff. So how much is your finance cost as a percent of sales, or your human resources cost, or your customer care cost as divided by your number of customers? You can work a thousand scenarios and different metrics. How many transactions do you conduct online versus your competitor or versus other vesting class companies?

When you do that, you will certainly find the good, the bad, and the ugly. Then you may target areas where you clearly can make improvements, and you're also likely to get some pushback. People say, "Well they're better because they're bigger, and they have more skill." You'll have to wrestle through those challenges.

Drive into your culture that you are about cost reduction and productivity each and every year. It's not something you do once and then you're done —it's something you're going to do on an ongoing basis. And you're going to benchmark yourselves every couple years, and you're going to target big opportunities, and you're also going to target many smaller opportunities.

How We Have Reduced Our Corporate Spending

We have reduced our corporate spending over the last year, as well as over the last five years.

Corporate and overhead costs, in general, which is principally corporate, have typically been easier to reduce, because they're bigger targets; they're allocated costs, things like information technology, finance, and human resources, and they're shared overhead costs. Those have been easier to reduce, because everybody recognizes them so much, and they're at least one step behind the customer.

Some other areas, such as customer care, sales, and marketing tend to be challenging. They're untouchable in some cases. "If we cut marketing, our revenues will collapse." I think that's the typical reaction in most organizations. The more removed you are from the customer, the more likely target you are for cost analysis.

I wouldn't say there are areas that simply cannot be trimmed, although that is situational. There are areas where you want to increase the investment, you want to grow, and there are other areas you say, "That's more of a harvest mode."

For us, we're adding retail stores. We'll add 200 retail stores this year. That's a lot of cost, particularly in the year you add them, because their same-store productivity tends to be low in the first year until they get up to speed and consumers know they're there. We feel we need to have a bigger retail presence, so we're adding those stores. Over a reasonably short period of time, it'll be economically positive; in the first year, it's not.

Cost-Cutting Decisions

Along with the business and functional leader, I help drive a lot of the spending decisions to lower levels, and that is done on the budget. If you squeeze them on the budget, they have to make those tradeoffs. But we set those budgets, so I do that along with the CEO and COO, and there are also places where I argue vehemently not to cut a budget.

It is hard to compare one organization to another as you determine appropriate funding levels for different parts of the business such as information technology or network versus our wireless business. It's really difficult. There are no great metrics for that; it's a mix of a little gut feeling instinct and a kind of situational sense of what is happening, and who has done a lot already, and who has kind of stayed out of the party.

Cost-cutting by itself is probably not a great tool. Cost-cutting combined with a focus on where you want to reinvest some of those resources and some of those savings, and how you want to change the business, is a lot more effective. It's pretty easy to just rip out cost, but you've got to run a business, too.

So, at the same time as you are taking down costs or increasing productivity, you have to drive growth, you have to drive customer care improvements, you have to ensure your product is meeting the needs of your customers. So that balance issue has to come in. Just doing less is not that valuable; doing more with less is real valuable, because that's productivity.

Once you've done some benchmarking and you've communicated the need for change, now with help from operational and functional people, they'll list the specific projects. We're going to change this process, or we're going to buy this system, or we're going to do something differently. Then you have to execute those, and you've got to monitor them regularly, possibly quarterly. How's this project going? Are we seeing the benefits we expected?

You may have to free up some funds to invest in those projects, particularly if it's a new system or process change. Then you need to track all those savings, and you've got to report them. You create visibility when you do that, because if all you do is hope someone is going to do what you've given them, you may wake up and find out they didn't do it; they've missed their budget, and there is no run-rate benefit because they haven't made a fundamental change.

I don't think this is rocket science; it's just pretty much blocking and tackling. It's the same kind of thing you do with any other strategic project in a business. You put together a plan, and you track it. You sign it out, and you create visibility around it.

Robert J. Dellinger assumed the role of executive vice president and chief financial officer of Sprint in June of 2002. Before joining Sprint, Mr. Dellinger was president and chief executive officer of GE Frankona Re based in Munich, Germany, with responsibility for General Electric's (GE) Employers Reinsurance Corporation's (ERC) European operations. ERC is one of the world's largest global reinsurers, with revenues of $3.7 billion and 1,300 employees across Europe.

During his GE career, Mr. Dellinger had diverse financial and operational experience in both GE industrial business and financial services, as well as extensive global experience, and he worked to grow these businesses. Other positions Mr. Dellinger held at GE include, starting in March of 1997, an officer of GE, and executive vice president and chief financial officer of ERC. In January of 1995, he was manager of finance for GE Motors and Industrial Systems, and in 1993 he was named director of finance and business development for GE Plastics Pacific, based in Singapore. From 1990 to 1993, he held various manager positions in the organization.

Mr. Dellinger joined GE in 1983 on the financial management program in consumer electronics business, moving, in 1985, to corporate audit staff and executive audit manager in 1989.

He graduated from Ohio Wesleyan University in 1982 with a B.A. in economics and a minor in accounting. He is a member of the Financial Executives Institute and served on numerous GE Plastics and GE ERC boards in Europe, Asia, and the United States. Most recently, he served on the boards of ERC, GE Frankona Re, GE Global Insurance Holdings, and ERC Life.

Keys to Being a Successful CFO

G. Marc Baumann

Executive Vice President, Chief Financial Officer, and Treasurer

Standard Parking Corporation

Areas of Focus

My position involves three basic functions:

1. First, we're a public company, so we need excellent internal control and financial reporting. This is first and foremost, and stands above everything else.

2. Second, I need to provide useful information and decision support. This means providing the right tools and templates; information technology reports to me, so we have all the routine processing that goes with our information technology systems. We need to provide information and analysis that can support the business organization. This is our analytical function: we provide everyone in the organization with templates for calculating return on investment and other financial metrics. This is in addition to the budget template support we provide to the operating side of the business to enable them to bid on contracts and create budgets for clients.

3. Third, I create productivity initiatives. This third function is all about doing things better, faster, and cheaper. That includes giving people the information they need to do their jobs, having strong controls, and helping the company achieve its profit goals by driving out cost. For example, we set out how can we reduce our general and administrative expense as a percentage of revenue, and we've reduced it dramatically in the time I've been here.

We view ourselves as a support function, so one of our goals is to help our organization change to be opportunistic. The outside world is changing all the time, and what our clients and customers want from us is constantly evolving. We need to be aware of those changes, and then help our organization take advantage of those opportunities. Clients and customers often make new demands on the organization, frequently for information or analysis, and our job is to ensure that the company is ready to respond to these demands.

Control, Creativity, and Balance

Being a successful chief financial officer is striking the right balance between supporting innovation and control. The operating people don't want a lot of controls; they want to be able to do what they think is best. We want them to think that way, to be encouraged to try new things and take chances. At the same time, we need control. We need to set some boundaries around what they do, while avoiding creating a command-and-control bureaucracy. Too much control stifles the organization in its ability to grow and be responsive to clients and customers. Too little control results in mistakes or fraud. The challenge for me is to make sure, in my area and throughout the business, we get that balance right.

Qualities and Ideology

The most important quality of a successful CFO is absolute integrity. That means doing the right thing regardless of the consequences for you or for the organization. You must never compromise your principles, however hard the decision. Sometimes that means recording liabilities people would rather you didn't, because it affects earnings. Integrity is first and foremost.

Second, a successful CFO must be fairly analytical and very comfortable with numbers, and also be able to communicate these financial ideas clearly. Most of the organization is not as financially astute as the people in finance and accounting, so you must be able to explain to them why things have to be done a certain way, and do so in terms they not only understand, but also buy into.

Last, a successful CFO must be able to sell ideas. The organization often views the CFO's ideas as restricting; CFOs are often required to change processes in ways that operations people feel limits their freedoms. You need to be able to make the rest of the organization see and understand the value of your changes, and understand that these changes actually help operations. The CFO must make the rest of the organization understand that the right control environment frees them up to do the things they want to do. It frees them from worrying about the potential for things to go wrong all the time.

I've been a CFO in manufacturing, in retail, in direct mail, in wholesale distribution, and now in business services. The challenges of the job are virtually identical across those industries. The basic challenges of control, information, reporting, and driving costs out apply to any business.

The skills I require of my team members are not unlike those required of a successful CFO. First of all, they need integrity. They have to be totally honest. They need to be analytical and comfortable with numbers. Almost every function in a business requires this comfort with numbers, whether you're in accounting and finance, or in operations, human resources, sales, or marketing. In my opinion, a successful business comes down to measuring according to numbers. I also require people who are good communicators. Perhaps most importantly, I look for people who are willing to tell me when they disagree with me. It's bad to be surrounded by nodding heads. I want people to challenge what I say and do—they should do it in a respectful way, of course, but if they don't agree, they should be willing to tell me why, and I need to encourage that type of conversation. I've spent most of my working life in the turnaround and restructuring of finance, accounting, and information technology functions. You need people who, when times are tough and big problems emerge, don't get worn down, and who have an inner resilience. I look for people who, when faced with adversity, embrace the challenge provided by it; people who get back up when they are figuratively knocked down, and are ready to try again and again.

My Strategies and Methodologies

I maintain a healthy skepticism about what's going on around me, whether in my own department or in other departments. I started out as an auditor working for one of the big firms, and they drill that into you: don't accept things at face value; always question things, and ask why it is this way and whether it makes sense.

I also spend a lot of time encouraging people to bring me bad news early, because the CFO in any business inevitably winds up dealing with the problems and mistakes. If people willingly bring you a small mistake, a suspicion, or a concern, you have the opportunity to take action and keep it from becoming something big. Then, when you find out about a problem or mistake, you have to be relentless in investigating it. You should investigate all problems and mistakes, correct them, and then do a root and branch investigation to get at the cause and determine the actions necessary to prevent it from happening again. You must:

1. Determine what happened. Go step by step through the sequence of events.
2. Identify what should have happened. What is the correct policy or procedure that should have been followed?
3. Compare what happened to the ideal.
4. Answer the question as to cause. Was it human error, breakdown of process, or lack of established policy or procedure?
5. Learn from that mistake.
6. Implement change in your policies, procedures, or processes to prevent the same thing from happening again.
7. Communicate the change, and train people in the new way of doing things.

Market Pressures and Internal Challenges

The CFO's number-one challenge is dealing with the tension between the financial market's pressure for predictability and the inherent uncertainty of future business performance in a competitive environment that is constantly changing. It's impossible to predict with absolute certainty how any business will perform. The reality of any business is that some things go better than expected and other things turn out worse than expected. These good and bad events are by definition unexpected. As the saying goes, "You don't know what you don't know." Therein lays the challenge. Trying to give the financial markets guidance on how we think the business is going to perform, against the backdrop of all the variability in any business, is the CFO's biggest challenge.

Handling this pressure starts with always questioning things, testing your own assumptions, and challenging your own and other people's thinking. When somebody gives you a financial projection, you don't just accept it. You must always be questioning, always testing out your thoughts and assumptions and what other people are telling you. Budgets and forecasts must be rigorously scrutinized. And it's vital to test assumptions through discussions with the chief executive officer and other key people. That's the only way to have the confidence to guide other's expectations for the business.

One major internal challenge is time. It's the one thing you can't get more of. If you're trying to live a balanced life, you can't work 24/7; you may be available 24/7, but you do want to have time for family and for other things in life besides work. It's a challenge to balance time commitments, because the organization has expectations: its various functional areas, the CEO, your own functional area, investors, and the board of directors all expect some of your attention and time. We all get more e-mail than we can possibly deal with, so it's a question of how you use your time.

The only way you can deal with it is to sit down and identify your priorities in advance. What are they going to be for the next month? What are they going to be for the next week? Every day before I leave, I sit down and confirm the one or two things I must accomplish tomorrow. It's not necessarily the thing that has the biggest deadline; it should be the thing that can have the most impact. I try to make an impact every day. I want to know it made a difference that I was here, that a problem got solved, or something was improved, or an important report or project was completed. I want to make certain we're always accomplishing things; pushing to do things better, faster, or more cost-effectively. The other stuff you just have to let go, because no one can do it all.

The other major internal challenge is when you have poor performance by someone on your team. We all know the right way to deal with performance issues: you start with written expectations so people are absolutely clear what to accomplish. If they're not meeting those expectations, you counsel them and give them an opportunity to improve with an agreed deadline, and hopefully they do improve. You really want them to improve and must support their efforts. Sometimes, they don't close the performance gap. You have to satisfy yourself that it's not because the organization didn't do its part in helping them succeed. Sometimes, we expect more of people than we should, because even the best person can fail if the expectations are unrealistic. You have to be satisfied that they were given a realistic chance to succeed. When all else fails, you have to take action. Sometimes that means letting people go and bringing in somebody else who can do the job in a better way. This is something you do reluctantly; it's difficult to do, but you have to be willing to do it. Ultimately, you cannot tolerate mediocre performance, because that contributes to a mediocre organization.

Executive Relationships and Communicating the Function

I work most closely with the CEO, but also with the general counsel, the corporate controller, and other senior executives. I also work closely with the executives in charge of operations, because in almost every business, finance and accounting are support functions; there's an operations function that constitutes what the business does every day to perform a service or make a product. It's key to form relationships with all of those people, particularly the operating people, because a lot of what the CFO does either supports them or requires things from them.

I begin these partnerships by finding out what the other executives need from me in order to excel at what they do. I also tell them what I need, so it's a two-way street. I am available for those senior people 24/7, so if they have a problem, issue, or question, or if they need something to satisfy a client or a customer, I am able to deliver a rapid response to their requests. That means your own functional area has to be available immediately to investigate any problems or issues that might arise. When somebody says, "I have a question. I can't figure this out," I immediately assign an analyst to it, and I try to deliver a response within a matter of hours or a day. People know they can come to me to get their questions answered or get the support they need. Of course, I expect the same response from them, and I can get it because I deliver it to them.

We have an acronym for our function called FAST, which stands for "Finance, Accounting, Strategy, and Technology." That is the totality of my responsibility. I tend to talk to people in the context of that acronym, because it helps people remember what we do and also connotes how we want to do it, which is fast. We want to be extremely responsive, and we want to help them win. We want to help them deliver what they need to their customer or client.

If we're not getting it done, we want to know about it and make sure we change how we do things so we are delivering. I frequently talk to people in operations and say, "If you're unhappy with anything in my area, call me and tell me about it." I don't say that just to the senior folks; I say it all the way down into the organization, so people know they can expect us to deliver for them. This means excellent processing of transactions and information, creating a proper control environment, managing an internal audit function, and delivering analytical support. We expect to deliver not according to our own terms, but according to their needs. If they are not having their needs met, they need to tell us, and we need to act and deliver what they need to succeed.

Setting Goals

The board of directors, along with executive management, determines the strategic vision for the company. The executive officers translate that vision into goals and plans to guide the company in the short and long term. Short-term planning involves the setting of goals to drive the company towards the achievement of its strategic vision.

The best way to do this is when senior management across all functions gets together and identifies the company's top goals for the year. Some of those goals will be applicable to my functional area, in that I can plan and implement the actions required to reach the goal independently of other functional areas. Other goals may require my functional area to help make change with or in other functional areas. For example, if there's a goal for another functional area to do something through technology, we will play a supporting role to support their efforts in achieving that goal.

I also have discussions with my direct reports concerning major areas where we think we can improve, either within our own area or in other departments. Then I ask, "Based on that information, what goals do you propose for yourself?" Ideally, if people propose their own goals, those goals are more likely to be achieved than if the goal is just handed to them; they actually believe in the goal and have committed to achieving it. In my experience, it is a myth that letting people set their own goals leads to less challenging goals. Usually, it's just the opposite, and I'm there to make sure the goals are SMART, which ensures the goal is a challenge, but also realistic. That's how goals are set, and this same approach cascades down through the organization. We then review progress periodically. I meet with all my direct reports for at least half an hour every two weeks. We meet many other times too, but we have a set meeting every two weeks just to review their progress toward their goals and to make time to discuss anything that could prevent the goals from being achieved.

Advice

The best piece of advice I give my team members is if you have an idea or change that you really believe in and it's rejected by the organization or by me, don't give up. If you really believe in it, come at it another time with another approach. Sometimes, a proposed change requires several attempts before people are comfortable with it. This is particularly true of significant changes. Sometimes an idea gets knocked down because it wasn't presented in the right way, because people had other things on their minds, or because it was presented a few months ahead of its time. Further analysis or quantifying additional benefits of the change is often all that is needed to gain acceptance. If I really believe we should do something, I never give up on it. You have to be a pit bull once in a while.

The best advice I've ever received is to never compromise your principles. It comes back to always doing the right thing. All the big frauds we read about in the newspaper came from people compromising their principles.

Growing Profits

In order to help the company grow the bottom line, the CFO must come in every day with the assumption that we can do a better job, that we can do the same job for less cost, that we can do it faster, that if we re-engineer how we do things, the business can become more efficient. Sometimes, this doesn't require re-engineering; sometimes it's a matter of fine-tuning. It does require a mindset that seeks continuous improvement in the way everything is done.

Always ask:

- How can the process be improved?
- How can we apply technology to make the process more automated and more efficient?
- Why do we do things the way we do? Is there a better way?

Always start with a blank piece of paper and outline a vision for the new desired state in the ideal world. This approach ensures that you aren't inhibited by the challenge of getting from where you are now to the new way of doing things. That can be considered later. Likewise, at this early stage, consider only the benefits and not the costs of the change. Again, the costs are important, but if considered prematurely, the estimates will be inaccurate, as the future state is not yet defined. Ballpark estimates are frequently wrong and if high, may prevent a serious consideration of the benefits, resulting in a decision to perpetuate the status quo.

The CFO must be a professional skeptic and not complacent or content with the way things are. He or she must never sit back and assume the business is a well-oiled machine requiring minimal attention. Success is a high-maintenance endeavor. This mindset guides everything I do. I come in every day and behave as though I have to prove myself like any new employee.

CFOs must also develop metrics beyond financial measures. People throughout all functional areas should report on how they're performing against targets and budgets, and should have easy access to information that shows trends and highlights whether performance is getting better or worse. If they're not getting better, people should be challenged to propose plans for improvement. Making sure we put metrics in place has a huge impact on results. Whatever gets measured gets improved. Metrics help the CFO shine a light on areas that need to improve. This includes providing leadership to the organization by first implementing and reporting metrics on the functional areas for which the CFO is responsible. Ultimately, the CFO's job is to make sure everyone has the information they need to succeed.

Team Expenses

In any service business, one of the greatest costs is payroll. When we have additional funds to spend, it's always spent on rewarding key performers, the people who exceed expectations consistently. We want to make sure those people are getting new challenges, and also are getting rewarded appropriately. We're always conscious of the competitive market that exists for top performers.

Another major expense is capital. We spend a lot of money on technology, and we exercise a lot of rigor to quantify the benefits of technology investment. There's a tendency to upgrade technology without sound financial reasons. If you just invest money in technology with the belief that it will be good, you will quickly find that requests far exceed resources and you have no objective means to judge the worthy projects from all the rest. We use return on investment criteria, and we have a cut-off we apply to our capital expenditures. That applies to every area of the business, and ensures that people do their homework and can justify how they spend money.

Research and Development

Internally, the most important elements of success for a CFO are really excellent relationships with senior operating executives, the CEO, the board of directors, the audit committee, the general counsel, and every other peer. It is imperative to have a great working relationship with those people, because they either know what's going on in the business in areas where you don't, or they have the power to change things that should be changed. I can't change anything in operations without convincing the senior operating people they should change it—unless I get the CEO to impose it, which is a poor strategy. On the external side, the biggest resources are quarterly meetings with the external counsel and auditors; organizations such as Financial Executives International; and conferences. The world outside your business is changing every day, and what your clients and customers expect from you changes all the time. Those who adapt and respond are able to take advantage of that change and thrive. It's easy to get complacent and start thinking you can reduce your business mode to a formula that is simply replicated each day. Even if done to a high standard, this approach will fail. One great quotation says, "Looking at all the failed companies, the only thing they did wrong was to keep doing that which made them successful a bit too long." In other words, they reduced their business model to a formula. And while this issue confronts the business as whole, it is no less true for the CFO's own areas of responsibility. You have to be adaptable, and that means being plugged into what's happening inside and outside the business, and being ready to change the way you do things.

We try to go to many conferences and talks. The senior executives frequently attend conferences and meetings with peers in other businesses or other industries, so we're aware of what's going on with our competitors and with companies in other industries. Many best practices emerge in industries other than your own. Financial Executives International is a terrific organization that puts on conferences on a regular basis.

There are other organizations, including the Association for Financial Professionals. This excellent organization is focused toward people in the treasury area and is a great resource. People at all levels, including those below the controller or the CFO, can benefit from this organization to find out what other businesses and what their peers are doing.

Perhaps by virtue of being a public company, we are deluged with cold calls from people with various organizations who want to sell us their products and services. It's easy just to dismiss them all, but if they sound intriguing, we do take the time to consider them, even if they would require radical change to how we do things. We force ourselves to think outside the box, and ask, "Could this new idea really transform our business or the way we operate our financial function?"

The Broadening Role of the CFO

People often think the CFO must be a human calculator. If ever I do a mental math calculation and get my decimal in the wrong place, people look at me with surprise—they assume I'm a bean counter, and that numbers are all that matter to me. CFOs have to be interested in everything that matters to the investment community. Some of these areas are numbers (Where is revenue going? Where is profit going?), but there's a lot behind the numbers. I can do a lot to help people succeed in their jobs besides just giving them a score card, and that's what I try to do. My job also requires me to say no to people fairly often; many times, I have to be the one to say, "The controls are not going to allow you to do that" or "Your proposal doesn't meet the return on investment criteria." I hope people don't assume I enjoy turning down proposals, when I'm just doing my job.

Sarbanes-Oxley has had a huge impact on the CFO's job description. It's the biggest thing to come down the tracks since Y2K. Y2K became an umbrella under which companies changed out their information technology systems and made a lot of changes in their processes; the same is true with Sarbanes-Oxley. People expect the CFO to drive that process, and that means taking on the sacred cows. We now have a greater reason to justify questioning established ways of doing business, and to say we can't do them that way anymore. Sarbanes-Oxley has helped us get our organization to buy into changes; internal control is now more fully embraced in all functional areas, because people now see the value of having stronger controls in the business. Previously, some resisted due to a narrow perspective that viewed strong internal controls as a shackle. They saw the costs of controls, but not the benefit. Sarbanes-Oxley has changed that, because now we have to do it. The role of the CFO is to beat the drum for strong internal controls. There's also an expectation by shareholders and boards of directors that the CFO will stand up, if necessary, to the CEO and make sure the right thing is done on accounting and disclosures.

The CFO's role historically revolved around accounting, financial reporting, and budgeting. Now, people are looking for a CFO who can help lead the company in the development of its strategy and in its overall corporate goal setting. Strategy is now part of the CFO's function. People now look at the CFO as someone with enough skill and knowledge to fill in for the CEO if need be. CFOs are no longer restricted to their functional silo of finance, accounting, or information technology; they are viewed as broad-based businesspeople who understand the business and how it works.

Two emerging trends are affecting the role itself. Technology is going to result in many fewer manual processes, which is a good thing, and fewer people as well. Finance and accounting functions will get smaller in terms of numbers of people; they will move away from people processing transactions, to knowledge workers doing analysis and using the outputs of the technology-driven process to help the business. The other trend is outsourcing. Certain functions within finance and information technology are going to get outsourced, and the CFO will put some of those relationships in place and manage them with less staff. Outsourcing, however, is a double-edged sword. On the one side, there is the significant savings and ability to leapfrog right to best practice processes. On the other side, there is the risk of colossal failure if the wrong outsourcers are chosen. The CFO role now requires the skills to successfully manage the selection of and transition to the outsource vendor.

The foundational rules of being a CFO, however, will never change. CFOs must always do the right thing, regardless of the impact on themselves or their organization. They must keep pushing to make things happen, and always manage on the assumption that there's always a way to do things better, faster, and cheaper.

G. Marc Baumann is responsible for all financial-related and information technology functions of Standard Parking Corporation. Prior to his appointment as chief financial officer for Standard Parking in 2000, Mr. Baumann was chief financial officer for Warburtons Ltd. in Bolton, England.

A Chicago native, Mr. Baumann joined Warburtons, Inc. in Chicago in 1989 as executive vice president and chief financial officer, and was promoted to the positions of president and chief executive officer in 1990. In 1993, Mr. Baumann relocated to England in connection with his appointment as chief financial officer of Warburtons Ltd., the third largest wholesale baker and distributor of fresh baked bread in the United Kingdom, a role in which he successfully restructured the firm's financial and information technology operations. Prior to his employment with Warburtons, Mr. Baumann was executive vice president and chief operating officer for Hammacher Schlemmer & Co.

Mr. Baumann is a certified public accountant in Illinois and a member of both the American Institute of Certified Public Accountants and the Illinois CPA Society. He holds a B.S. degree from Northwestern University, and an M.B.A from the Kellogg School of Management at Northwestern University.

The CFO: Assets and Revenue Safeguard

Scot J. Farrell

Chief Administrative Officer
Wilmer Cutler Pickering Hale and Dorr LLP

The CFO's Primary Role in a Law Firm Environment

Large law firms, in particular large law firm partnerships, have a uniquely different structural environment, especially when compared to a private corporation or a public company. In a corporation, you have a chief executive officer who answers to either the board of directors and the shareholders or to a small group of private owners. That CEO is responsible for the success of the organization because of a vision and how he or she manages the rest of the organization to attain that vision. In attaining that vision, a clear organizational structure is established with the C-level managers being given the authority needed to accomplish their portion of the vision. This allows the corporation to move in tandem, focusing on the goals that have been set out.

In a large law firm partnership, the CEO, who is quite often referred to as the managing partner or chairman of the management or executive committee, also has the responsibility of vision and direction for the firm. But, responsibility for vision and direction is only one small part of the picture, since the law firm CEO is also tasked with managing the individual idiosyncrasies of the partners/owners. Managing lawyers in a partnership is best described by the phrase, "it's like herding cats." Large law firm lawyers are a group of highly charged, self-motivated, well-trained, and educated individuals, each of whom have strong opinions as to the steps necessary to achieve the firm's success and their personal success. These opinions are quite often in direct opposition to the vision of the law firm's CEO and, therefore, force the law firm CEO to spend an inordinate amount of time building consensus among the partners/owners of the firm.

In a law firm, the organizational structure is not the standard design where the CEO is sitting at the top with all of the other C-level positions answering specifically to the CEO. Most law firms use a committee approach for accomplishing the goals that have been set out by management, and the chief financial officer becomes an active participant in the decision-making process of each committee. The CFO in this situation is charged with the responsibility of safeguarding the firm's assets and revenue stream, and must do so by helping each committee come to the correct consensus. There will always be a question as to what exactly is the correct consensus, since business decisions in law firms quite often have a fair amount of emotion involved in the process. This emotion should not be taken as a negative, since the majority of the partners I have worked with over the years will worry about how a committee and firm decision will affect a myriad of subjects such as the morale of the staff and associates, the outside world's perception of the firm, clients' perception of the firm, the financial success of the firm, and so on. Committee-based decisions are not only based on a preponderance of the facts involved, but also on how those decisions affect individual partners' business and personal lives.

In the law firm I work for, there are approximately 320 owners, and each owner has a vote in the decisions that are made (one person, one vote). Under those circumstances, you're not working in a standard hierarchy; you're working in an environment that requires consensus. To be successful as the CFO, you must be agile and able to work with various diverse personalities—some very strong, some not—while still helping to achieve financial success and the chairman's vision of the future.

The relationship that exists between the CFO and the CEO tends to be more of a consultative role whereby ideas are exchanged on how to achieve success and a consensus is established on how to approach the partnership. My job is to keep the firm focused on its financial needs, and to keep the firm focused on how to improve profitability without destroying the fabric that makes the firm what it is. This requires me to explain to each and every partner the financial cost or benefit of a transaction and the non-financial exposures a decision might create. For example, law firms tend to be very generous, beyond market benchmarks, to employees regarding vacation and sick day allowances. Under the assumption that the firm wanted to reduce expenses in order to help make it more financially attractive to laterals, I would make a proposal to reduce the allowances so they are more in line with the benchmarks. I would also have to be in a position to discuss how this will affect employee morale, what the risks were of employee flight, what the cost savings would be in reducing the allowances, what unforeseen costs we would incur due to employees being disgruntled, how this would reduce our ability to recruit, what would happen and what would be the cost if we decided to increase our allowances instead of decrease, and so on.

Throughout the committee discussion of our desire to reduce allowances to market levels, my staff and I have to be knowledgeable regarding every possible permutation for change the committee could think of, even though, logically, the decision to reduce the allotment should be fairly simple, assuming the rest of the firm's benefits are at or above benchmarks. A law firm's CFO's role here is to keep the committee focused on the goal of reducing the allotment and how that reduction will improve the firm's profitability. The communication of the allotment change will require a significant amount of communication to the staff as to why the change must occur and how their participation in that change will help the firm's overall success. The staff may not be happy about the proposed changes, but they do understand and respect the need for business to be successful relative to market peers.

In a law firm, the way you make your money is hours multiplied by the rate charged to a client. The profitability of our client relationships is further enhanced based on the firm's ability to push the work down to the lowest ranking timekeeper who can perform the work and prepare the client-requested work product in an accurate and professional manner. Like any service industry company, the higher the level of leverage (ratio of non-partner timekeeper hours worked on a matter compared to partner timekeeper hours) you can achieve, the better your chances are for increased profitability. The only way to greatly improve income/profitability is to either increase the average hours worked per timekeeper per year, or to increase the leverage. Keep in mind that increasing leverage alone without making sure timekeepers are properly utilized is a recipe for failure.

You can try to increase the hourly rates charged to clients, but there is such pressure nowadays to control your rates or to give even greater amounts of discounts, that the ability to have elasticity in the rates charged is almost nonexistent. In recent years, clients have made it excruciatingly clear that there is a limit as to how much they are willing to pay for a standard line partner. If you're an individual who is renowned in your field, and your legal practice has the ability to attract "bet the company" type cases, the rates you are able to charge are completely and totally elastic. Otherwise, you're looking at a market with very limited elasticity for rate increases and an environment where clients are saying, "I'm not willing to pay you much more than $XXX an hour for somebody with ten or fifteen years of partner experience."

One of the other responsibilities of the CFO is to help management focus on how to improve profitability by analyzing the clients you have, the value the firm receives for the client relationship, and the client's financial contribution to the firm, using a cost accounting methodology that establishes individual client and matter profitability. Cost accounting methodologies in law firms are fairly new. Law firms have not historically looked at the financial contributions a client makes to the firm using a model for relative comparison of one client to another. They have not reviewed their "book of business" and said, "Gee, this set of clients or this practice is not making the kind of contribution, financially or otherwise, we would like our clients to make. Therefore, we are going to disengage from that client."

In doing that analysis, a significant amount of data has to be acquired about your client and the matters assigned. You will need to know in detail the individuals who have worked on the matters, the hours they have spent on the client, and the total hours they have charged to any client. You will need to know the fully loaded cost of the timekeepers involved in the firm's overhead costs, and any other direct costs associated with the client under analysis. In creating this profitability model, you will compare the cost of performing the work assigned by the client to the revenue generated to determine the matters, the clients, profitability, etc.

The risk of doing profitability analysis, as described above, is the fact that the busiest person in the firm becomes the most sought after timekeeper; every hour you add to their total hours charged to clients reduces the cost of having them work on a matter, thereby increasing the matter's profitability. The CFO must now educate the partners and management that you obtain similar results by increasing the workload of any timekeeper, not just the busiest. Further, it becomes absolutely necessary to control workload allocations so the firm's best and highly utilized attorneys are not disenfranchised to the point of quitting. Therefore, the profitability models will require several variances, including looking at client matters based on overall firm averages of hours and costs. This will allow a client matter to be assigned to anyone who is not highly utilized, over compensated, etc.

Adding Value

In addition to the responsibility for helping the firm maintain and improve profitability and properly prepare and explain financial data, the CFO must keep careful control of the firm's balance sheet. According to Citibank, banker to eighty of the Am Law 100 law firms, partnership capital should be approximately 10 percent of annual gross revenue. Therefore, if a firm has $500 million in annual revenue, that firm's total capital value should be approximately $50 million. This 10 percent balance allows law firms to have sufficient enough cash flow throughout the year so borrowings are short-term and minimal. Most law firms receive the majority of their cash receipts in the last half of the year (with December collections being the most significant). In order to pay those expenses that are incurred throughout the year, such as payroll, lease obligations, etc., the firm should retain sufficient cash to cover the regular and ongoing expenses. Borrowings should be limited to and used for unexpected expenses and capital improvements.

Though many law firm CEOs would cringe at this comment, borrowings should never be used to make distributions to the partners. When law firms borrow to make distributions of income to partners, they are betting on the partners being sufficiently motivated to collect outstanding receivable. A much more efficient motivation process is to only pay distributions to the partners when there is sufficient cash flow. There is no better motivation for a partner to collect outstanding receivables than to know that if he and his follow partners do not collect outstanding balances, there will be no distributions. When I meet new partners and talk to them about law firm finances, I explain to them an accounting method I refer to as the CIF method of accounting. Unlike GAAP accounting or LIFO and FIFO inventory tracking systems, the CIF method of accounting is simple and easy: "If the Cash is not In my Fist, you do not get paid."

Another area of responsibility for a law firm CFO is to minimize the firm's exposure to taxes, both nationally and internationally. This requires a full understanding of the tax laws of each one of the United States, and the foreign countries in which the firm transacts business. The CFO has to know how international tax laws and treaties interrelate to the United States tax laws. Without this knowledge or without the ability to access this knowledge through one of the major international accounting firms, law firms will and do create significant exposures. For example, there are tax treaties that will allow a firm to take advantage of transfer pricing and overhead allocations to a foreign location, but if you do not follow the documentations rules of a specific country, your advantageous deduction will be disallowed and your tax burden in the foreign jurisdiction will significantly increase. Something as simple as not maintaining statutorily required receipted support for an allocation of overhead into a country such as Belgium can result in what was originally a $1 million reduction of Belgium source revenue becoming $500,000 or more in additional Belgium taxes. Further, a complete understanding is needed of how a tax transaction in one country affects how the United States Internal Revenue Service views that transaction. Again, a tax favorable treatment in a foreign jurisdiction could be well received by the partners who are resident in that foreign jurisdiction, but the United States Internal Revenue Service treatment of that transaction could result in all of the firm's partners paying higher taxes in the United States. Even though United States tax rates are one of the lowest in the world, there are foreign jurisdictions where income is not recognized in the same manner as in the United States. This can result in favorable foreign tax treatments, because the taxes are applied against a smaller income base, but at a higher tax rate. This could easily result in less taxes than would have to be paid in the United States. Therefore, the CFO must be able to identify possible exposures and learn how to play the international tax balancing game.

Further, because we are a United States-based law firm, it is important to recognize as much foreign tax credit as possible. In doing so, we have to focus on the physical jurisdiction of where the work of our attorneys is being completed. We need to know how much of that work is being done in foreign countries and foreign locations, and how much of that work we can truly assign to a country in which we don't have a tax exposure. By maintaining detailed records of physical jurisdictions, you are able to source income as foreign source income without subjecting it to foreign taxes, thereby allowing the partners to take a greater amount of foreign tax credits and reduce their United States tax obligations.

The CFO's role at a law firm is not only to look at the financial well being of the firm, but also to determine how that financial well-being interrelates with the other departments and disciplines within the firm. How can that

CFO support legal personnel, human resources, marketing, the lawyers' practice of law, etc.? How can the CFO accomplish the goals of each one of the individual practice areas of a large multinational law firm while still keeping an eye on the bottom line?

Like in any business, the CFO of a law firm has to understand that the accomplishment of the CEO's vision and goals is a marathon race and not a wind sprint. Law firms have to make investments in their infrastructure, knowing those investments may not show a return for many years to come. A growing law firm will need additional staff such as secretaries, legal assistants, billers, reprographics assistants, etc., long before the hiring of additional attorneys. Without having the support staff in place prior to the arrival of new attorneys, you will be not able to have that new revenue producer working efficiently on day one. Therefore, the CFO works with management and the CEO to focus on the fact that expenses will increase at a faster rate of growth than revenue. As soon as the growth slows for a short period of time, the reverse will happen and revenue will grow at a significantly faster rate than expenses did during the growth period (unless, of course, the slowdown in growth is due to a slowdown in the firm's business).

A Successful CFO

In a law firm, a CFO needs to be a generalist, and a good businessperson. The old-fashioned blood and guts accountant who is well versed in the rules for generally accepted accounting will do well in the preparation of financial data and analysis, but if that CFO does not have an overall understanding of the business of practicing law, he will not be successful. You need to understand the changes occurring daily in the law firm industry. You need to understand human nature, since the biggest portion of your job is dealing with people. But most of all, you need to be able to establish personal relationships with the partners, attorneys, and staff of the firm. These personal relationships become the foundation for helping establish the consensus that was discussed previously. Keep in mind that it is easier to agree with someone if you have a personal relationship with him or her and trust his or her judgment.

The fact that I'm a CPA helps in identifying areas of financial and accounting concern, but my CPA background does absolutely nothing for me in understanding how lawyers act and react. The understanding of lawyers comes with time, experience, and a fair amount of patience. If you perform a search of the internet regarding the psychology of lawyers, you will find over a hundred articles, each one claiming to understand how lawyers think, act, and arrive at decisions. Lawyers are no different than any other group of very competitive individuals who are trained to think quickly and be argumentative. As the CFO, you must learn to think just as quickly as the lawyers do, you must learn to avoid arguments, and most of all you must learn not to let the lawyers see you sweat. Confidence in your knowledge and abilities is a key to your success, along with one hell of a sense of humor.

A successful CFO participates in all aspects of the firm, from attorney and staff recruiting, to operations and facilities management, to marketing and business development. When the CFO helps the various firm managers interview or orient new employees, he or she is gaining a better base for understanding the needs of the staff and the future direction of the firm. Participation in operations and facilities helps the CFO understand the basic support necessary to allow the revenue producers to be successful. Participation in projects relating to marketing and business development help the CFO understand changes in the firm's client's industries and how those changes will ultimately affect the legal industry.

Challenges

The biggest challenge for any law firm administrator, whether it's the chief financial officer, the chief marketing officer, the chief technology office, or even the chief human resources officer, is dealing with attorneys on a day-to-day basis. All of the attorneys I have dealt with throughout my twenty-year law firm administrator career have been honors graduates from the top law schools in the country: Harvard, Yale, Columbia, Stanford, Chicago, UVA, Michigan, etc. As stated earlier, these graduates are extremely intelligent lawyers who have been trained to find flaws in arguments and use those flaws to their advantage when debating. Therefore, when a decision is made that modifies the status quo of the firm, an administrator will inevitably be confronted by at least one attorney, if not more, who is uncomfortable with the decision. You then find yourself having to explain the decision-making process and justify the result. This is after you have already gone through the same process with either a committee of partners or the firm's management committee. I applaud law firms for their open debates, for their giving all individuals associated with the firm the right to debate a decision. I would never want to change that philosophy, but it does wear one down, and therefore creates a significant challenge.

From a CPA's prospective, the accounting and reporting process in a law firm is very easy. Most law firms keep their books on a cash basis, modified cash basis, or tax basis. Most transactions are recorded only when either a check is cut or a cash receipt is recorded. All time inventory and accounts receivable is maintained off balance sheet. The real complexity and challenge in the accounting portion of the CFO's position is the allocation of net income to each of the partners based on their ownership sharing percentages. The reason this becomes complex and challenging is that most firms allocate income on a daily prorate basis (throughout the year), no matter when the cash is actually received. Therefore, income allocations are affected by the addition and termination of partners during the year. Income allocations are further complicated by special agreements (bonuses, cost of living adjustments, mid-year income sharing adjustments, etc.) or guaranteed payments granted by the management committee of the firm. In a law firm of 300 partners, you will have a minimum of 109,500 calculations to be made over a 365-day year.

Prior to any committee discussions regarding a change at the firm, it is essential for the CFO to "walk the halls and plant seeds." The need for consensus building requires that private one-on-one conversations take place where the CFO obtains input from various partners who are viewed as firm leaders. This input gives you invaluable information as to how the partnership might react, and it allows you to modify the proposal so consideration is given to the input received.

With the modifications, a significantly higher level of probability exists for the proposal to be accepted by management and the partnership as a whole.

Setting Goals

Annually, our firm goes through a firm-wide goal- and objective-setting process. During this process, we determine how the firm is going to grow and how that growth ties into the CEO's vision for the future. Each administrative and legal department participates in the preparation of a firm-wide budget. Included in that budget is a detailed listing of the expenses we anticipate will be incurred during the year. A subset of the attorney expenses is a detailed listing of how the firm expects to grow through the addition of new and lateral hire attorneys, offset by attorney attrition.

For the past ten years, intellectual property law has been a very hot area, so law firms with a desire to build an intellectual property practice focused on hiring lateral hires and new graduates from law school who had science-related undergraduate degrees. If you were smart about your hiring needs, you found a few lawyers who could handle patent prosecution and a few lawyers who were quite capable in handling patent litigation cases. Some firm's met their needs by acquiring or merging with patent law boutiques, which tended to be a less costly venture, but did not allow the acquiring firm to cherry-pick the attorneys that were deemed as being high-profile. As other practice areas saw their case loads diminish, the attorneys in those practice areas found themselves going through a retraining process whereby they had originally started their careers as environmental or medical malpractice defense litigators, and they now began the process of training to be patent litigators.

The goal-setting process allows a firm to review where it has excess capacity and where attorneys are working at breakneck paces, requiring a significant infusion of help. It is the CFO's responsibility to make suggestions to the CEO as to how the firm can move individuals from areas with excess capacity to those areas that are over capacity. The difficulty with moving individual attorneys between practices is whether the background and training they currently have is compatible and supportive to the group looking for help.

Once the initial goal- and objective-setting process is completed and the firm's annual budget process is finalized, it is presented to management for final approval and implementation.

CEO and CFO: Working Together

Law firm CEOs do not fit into a single mold. Some CEOs are pure visionaries, spending their time focusing on the future direction of the firm and the steps that are necessary in order for the firm to achieve the vision. Other CEOs are focused only on improving profitability. Profitability improvements may not require the CEO to establish a vision of the future. Instead, the CEO focuses on key financial statistics (such as utilization, realization, leverage, productivity, etc.) and how the firm can improve its performance. In either case, the CFO must be available to the CEO to help accomplish the standards desired and model the results that will be achieved.

Several years ago, I worked for a CEO at a southwest firm who had the vision of establishing an east and west coast presence through a merger. Since at this time very few significant mergers had been accomplished, benchmarking information was not available to help us create a visionary model that could be supported in facts. Instead of focusing on historic information, we decided to create a model of what the desired firm would look like and how that modeled firm would affect the combined firm's bottom line. As I am sure you can guess, this visionary model resulted in a positive contribution to the combined firm, and the initial investment made by both firms to realize the merger was recouped within one year. In truth, when the actual merger candidate was determined, it looked nothing like the firm that was modeled, and the financial results were far less spectacular than the modeled financial results. The good news is that the vision, slightly modified, was the correct vision, and the acquisition of a New York and Los Angeles presence as part of a merger was the most efficient way to set up offices in those locations. The bad news was that the initial cost to merge the firms and the resulting losses that occurred subsequent to the merger took five or more years to recoup.

More recently, I spent time with the CEO of my current employer, focusing on the preparation of an infrastructure model. This model was focused on the firm's need to increase capital. As stated earlier, Citibank's benchmark survey disclosed that a capital value equal to 10 percent of gross revenue was most desirable, and the most profitable firms in the United States had capital values that tended toward the 10 percent goal. Through the creation of a model, the CEO and I were able to put in place a plan to move the firm toward the 10 percent goal. Over a period of two years where the firm's income exceeded our annual plan, we were able to take that excess income and invest it into the firm rather than distribute the cash to the partners. This improvement in capital also helped the firm to be an attractive candidate for a merger. On May 31, 2004, the law firms of Wilmer Cutler Pickering LLP and Hale and Dorr LLP merged to become Wilmer Cutler Pickering Hale and Dorr LLP, one of the fifteen largest law firms in the United States with combined income in the range of three quarters of a billion dollars.

Saving Money and Decreased Expenses

Saving money for the firm is one of the CFO's primary responsibilities. The CFO, by nature, should be conservative, wanting to reduce expenses or at least be certain with a high level of assurance that every expense dollar spent results in the firm receiving revenue at a greater level of return than the dollar expended. The three most significant costs at a law firm are attorney compensation and benefits, support staff compensation and benefits, and lease costs. These expense categories generally represent 80 percent of a firm's total annual expenses. Therefore, the low-hanging fruit for expense cutting is clearly attorney and staff costs. The cutting of attorneys, unless an attorney is continually underutilized, is foolish, since in most instances an attorney contributes to the firm's profitability after the second year. The next target to focus on is support staff. If the ratio of the firm's support staff to attorney timekeepers is greater than one to one, there are distinct possibilities for savings by cutting excess staff. The CFO and the firm's management committee, which is chaired by the CEO, should continually review opportunities for cutting expenses and saving money. It is the CFO's and the CEO's fiduciary responsibility to make sure the assets of the firm are being used in an efficient, revenue producing manner.

Throughout history, there has never been a law firm that has been able to cut expenses into prosperity. The key to saving money is to increase revenue. Every dollar you increase revenue, in excess of fixed costs, results in a greater long-term contribution to the firm's profitability. Law firms and law firm partners require a significant support network in order to practice law. This network consists of lawyers, paralegals, library staff, research assistants, technology staff, recruiters, marketers, etc. Each support unit and the functions they perform allow attorneys to focus on the practice of law, and the practice of law is where revenue is produced. Therefore, it does not make a lot of sense for a partner to create a marketing plan when marketing staff are available to do so. The partner should focus on using his or her time for servicing current clients and developing new ones.

The hardest decision for any law firm to make is whether to ask a partner to withdraw from the firm. Except for a partner who is in his or her first few years as a new partner or a partner whose productivity is in the 2,500 hour a year range, partners are not generally contributors to the firm's bottom line. If an average partner earns $700,000 per year and that partner's overhead is $300,000, the partner must generate at least a $1,000,000 per year in revenue just to cover his or her costs. If the partner works 1,800 client hours at a rate of $500 per hour, the partner generates only $900,000 of revenue, resulting in a shortfall of $100,000. Of course, in most major law firms, this shortfall is covered by the excess contribution produced by associates (which points out the importance of leverage and proper utilization levels for associates).

If a partner is not producing in the form of client service hours, "rain making," or valued service to the internal workings of the firm, the CEO, the CFO, and the management committee must recommend to the firm the termination of that partner. As said earlier, this will be one of the hardest decisions management will ever make. Management must be well versed in all of the statistical data that can be produced regarding each partner's practice, contributions to the firm, both monetarily and otherwise, and relationship within the community. The CFO should be available for the CEO and other partners involved in this termination decision so the analytical data can be properly interpreted. Further, the CFO must support the CEO and the management committee's decision, no matter how the decision-making process concludes.

The firm can focus on the remaining 20 percent of expenses as an area where cuts can be implemented. There is no doubt in my mind that every law firm can do a better job of managing these smaller expense items and obtain significant results. It is the CFO's responsibility to identify those line items that are candidates for cutting and, in partnership with the CEO and the management committee, put into place procedures that will help the firm realize the benefits. This process should be continuous and ongoing throughout the year. Whether the process involves the renegotiation of firm-wide supply purchase contracts or the discontinuance of an employee perk, there are expenses that can be cut. The issue with making these cuts is the perception that the firm is being penny-wise and pound-foolish. Though the partners will be the financial benefactors of these expense reductions, they are quite often the first to complain that the cuts are not necessary.

Increasing Profits

In a law firm, there are three lowest common denominators - expenses, timekeepers, and matters. We have already discussed expense cutting and the benefits that can be derived from a systematic review of expenses. We have also discussed that the revenue stream for a law firm comes from the charging of time, by a timekeeper, at a specific rate to a client. The one item we have not discussed is the relationship of timekeepers to the client matters on which they work, and how the firm can improve profitability by making minor modifications to the mix of timekeepers for a matter, or by replacing less profitable client matters with more profitable ones. To accomplish this analysis, a profitability model has to be built.

The profitability model is based on the rules that govern cost accounting. Data must be collected that allows the CFO to determine the direct and indirect cost per hour for each timekeeper that works on a matter. Therefore, the analysis starts with the acquisition of timekeeper salary data, benefits costs, employee relations costs, other indirect employee costs, prorata lease and lease space costs, client marketing costs, and an allocation of the firm's overhead costs that are not specifically identifiable to a client. With this information, you are able to determine the cost of every hour charged to that client's matters and how the revenue derived from the client is calculated. You are also able to determine the time value of money associated with the client.

Does it take the firm thirty or sixty days to render a monthly bill to the client? How long does it take for the client to pay the monthly bill rendered by the firm? Is there work being performed on the matter that should be handled by an associate rather than a partner, or by a paralegal rather than an associate (leverage)? Can you increase the rates being charged by a specific class of timekeepers since the work they are performing is of a significant benefit to the client and is using a valuable resource of the firm? Does the client receive a discount on this matter, and is that discount justified by the work being performed, either at the matter level or at the overall client level? Clients who have a significant amount of work to be performed often receive discounts from law firms in order for the law firm to get all of the client's available legal work. In other instances, discounts are given to clients because the work being performed on a matter involves a group of timekeepers who have excess capacity.

After all of the questions have been answered and the true profitability of the client and the client's matters have been calculated, the firm now has the ability to determine if the continued relationship of the firm and the client makes financial sense. If the work being performed is in an area of law where excess capacity exists and the termination of the client's work will result in further increases in excess capacity, it is clear and prudent to continue working for that client. On the other hand, if the work being performed is in an area of law that is significantly over capacity and the contribution being created by that work is not commensurate with the benefit derived, the firm should consider modifying the pricing structure involved. If the client is unwilling to make modifications and the firm has enough work "in back order" to replace the hours expended, consideration should be given to discontinuing any future work for that client.

Merger Candidate Buying Decisions: The CFO and Management

In the law firm environment, when a merger discussion is ongoing, the discussion always starts with management focusing on issues regarding compatibility between the firms. Law firms tend not to focus, first and foremost, on dollars and cents in the initial stages of a merger. There are too many instances where law firms merged for the sake of money and ultimately blew apart. Smart mergers are based on the firms' desire to enhance their practices, expand into new and complimentary practice areas, or to find a firm that will compliment and expand the type of law practiced by the firm.

Perhaps your firm does not have a strong corporate practice, so you go and look to acquire a corporate practice that will support the growth desired. The discussion regarding a possible merger starts first at the CEO level and then works its way through the firm's management committee. The CFO gets involved at the point where it is necessary to perform due diligence and determine if the firms are financially compatible. To merge together a law firm in which the average partner makes $1 million a year with a law firm where the average partner makes $500,000 a year is a recipe for failure. The disparity of incomes alone will tend to create jealousy between the firms. If jealousy does exist, the partners and staff of both firms will spend valuable client time focusing on this issue rather than on ways to integrate the firms. Further, those individuals who are of marketable quality at the lower average partner compensation firm will be cherry-picked by headhunters taking advantage of the dysfunctional environment that now exists.

Another area of concern is the basic work ethic of the firms considering the combination. If both firms have the expectation that every lawyer will work 2,000 hours a year, then both firms have a common work ethic and compatibility. If the firms have as little as a 200-hour difference in what they believe to be a fair level of utilization and production, and neither firm is willing to amend their hours targets, the firms will have an issue regarding compatibility. Again, when there is a question regarding compatibility and the firms are unstable, a high risk of failure exists.

Scot J. Farrell is a proven leader, capable of maintaining a high level of effectiveness and flexibility while managing rapid change. He has served since 2001 as director of business planning, CAO, and CFO of Wilmer Cutler Pickering Hale and Dorr LLP. He is responsible for firm worldwide policies and procedures that affect attorney administrative, financial, and operational support departments. Wilmer Cutler Pickering Hale and Dorr LLP is an American Lawyer "A-List" international limited liability partnership with cash receipts in excess of $800 million. Mr. Farrell assisted in the 2004 merger of *the law firms of Wilmer Cutler Pickering LLP of Washington, D.C. and Hale and Dorr LLP of Boston, one of the largest mergers in legal history.*

Before joining Wilmer Cutler Pickering Hale and Dorr, Mr. Farrell opened and established a financially successful branch office of Driver Resource Company, Inc. in Houston, Texas. From 1986 to 2000, he served as CFO of Fulbright & Jaworski LLP, where he managed all administrative and financial review procedures regarding mergers and acquisitions. This responsibility included due diligence on two significant mergers (1989 and 1999) and multiple other smaller acquisitions and mergers. Due diligence was performed in Hong Kong in a 1990 acquisition of a Pacific Rim presence. From 1981 to 1985, he served as supervising accountant to Coopers & Lybrand International.

Adding Value and Ensuring Financial Integrity

Alfred H. Drewes

Senior Vice President and Chief Financial Officer
The Pepsi Bottling Group, Inc.

Creating a Financial Impact

One of the first things I did upon joining the Pepsi Bottling Group (PBG) back in 2001 was to work with the leadership of the finance organization to develop our mission and the operating principles that would guide our actions. Drawing upon the collective years of experience and considerable breadth of knowledge of my leadership team, we looked to provide the entire organization with a distinct sense of purpose and clear objectives.

Today, my organization has a very clear mission. We focus on creating value for PBG. This notion of creating value is the mindset I would like my organization to have as it executes its day-to-day activities.

We also identified four critical operating principles that support our mission of creating value for the company. These principles provide absolute clarity about what we as a finance organization must achieve each and every day. Our four operating principles are:

1. Ensure financial integrity and stewardship.
2. Drive insights, build financial literacy.
3. Deliver our commitments.
4. Respect each other.

Ensure Financial Integrity and Stewardship

The starting point for any financial organization is ensuring the integrity of a company's financials and providing stewardship over the company's assets. It is our job to ensure that the company is operating within both the letter and the spirit of the law and regulatory requirements. This is not a grey area—integrity is black and white. You either have it or you don't. At PBG, operating with integrity is non-negotiable.

At the same time, we have a responsibility to identify and capitalize on opportunities to help the company operate more efficiently, to grow and to prosper. By utilizing our expertise in specific functions, such as tax, treasury or strategic planning, and partnering with our general management population, we can find ways to generate more value for our company's shareholders.

As with all publicly traded companies, the responsibilities of ensuring financial integrity and providing stewardship have grown substantially in recent years in terms of the quantity of work required as well as the complexity of that work. Whether it's the heightened reporting requirements of Sarbanes-Oxley, the challenges posed by Regulation Fair Disclosure (Reg FD), the increased dialogue between management and our audit committee, or more complex reporting and disclosure rules, all of these have placed heightened demands on the finance organization.

At PBG, we approach this work using the same framework as creating value for the company. While everyone recognizes that we're obligated by law to complete this work, our challenge is to ensure that we're doing so in a way that also enhances our business. We want to find ways to drive shareholder value through enhanced regulatory compliance and corporate governance.

The additional scrutiny created by these new requirements has helped us to refine the way we operate. Specifically, we've had the opportunity to partner with our operating managers in new ways, becoming even more involved in the daily operations of the company.

For example, the process discipline required by Sarbanes-Oxley has enabled us to enhance certain internal controls in the company. It has brought a laser-like focus to the components of our margins and operating expenses. This focus has enabled our line operating managers to improve the financial performance of their particular area of the business. Through this process, we have not only met our fiduciary responsibilities, but we've been able to use this exercise to actually create added value for the company.

Another example is the increased level of dialogue between PBG management and our board of directors, particularly with the audit committee. PBG has always had an active board, but as with every other publicly traded company, the breadth of the discussion has increased substantially over the past few years. I believe this is a very positive development in two ways.

First, it helps the board fulfill its increasingly demanding oversight responsibilities. Second, we view it as an opportunity to draw upon the wealth of experience individual board members bring to PBG. This is just another way in which we can drive value for the company while at the same time meet a fiduciary responsibility.

Drive Insights, Build Financial Literacy

PBG is the world's largest manufacturer, seller, and distributor of Pepsi beverages. In the United States, we have operations in forty-one states. We also operate in Canada, Mexico, Greece, Russia, Spain, and Turkey. The bottling business is very operationally intensive. With nearly 65,000 employees around the world, there are literally thousands of decisions being made each and every day that affect our volume produced and sold, our revenue, and our costs. It is our job in the finance function to make sure the people making those decisions understand the financial implications of their choices. Financial literacy is all about providing tools and guardrails for our employees to guide their decision making.

In our business, margin management is extremely complex. It is the single most important profit driver. It requires an in-depth understanding of all the levers we can pull across our vast portfolio of products to maximize our profitability.

A few short years ago, our business wasn't so complicated. We could hire a great salesperson and send them into a customer to sell as much Pepsi as possible. But the world and our business is not the same today. Our portfolio has exploded in terms of new products and packages. Our customer base has become far more diverse and sophisticated. And our sales force collectively conducts several hundreds of thousands of customer interactions each and every day.

Today, when a consumer enters a typical supermarket in the United States, he or she will find a wide array of Pepsi products on the shelves and in various coolers throughout the store. These products come in several different packages, all with unique price points. If that same consumer walks into a convenience store, he or she will encounter a completely different set of SKUs at different price points. And, of course, when that individual goes to a local deli or pizza restaurant, there's yet another set of product options and price points. Each of these products and price points is individually tailored to the consumer that shops in that kind of outlet, and whether they intend to consume the product immediately or in the future.

Multiply those simple examples by the thousands of supermarkets, convenience stores, and restaurants across the country, and you begin to realize just how complex margin management is in the bottling business. We must determine the right price point for each of these products in each location in a way that optimizes our volume and profit growth.

The pricing of our products is quite dynamic. The process we use to make those pricing decisions is very intricate. We don't simply decide we're going to take our prices up a set amount on January 1st across the country. We need to evaluate all of the market dynamics for each product, in each store, in each of PBG's territories.

The finance organization is an invaluable partner in this process. We generate business and market insights for the business leaders conducting those evaluations, and we build the organization's financial literacy by providing the right tools and guardrails. This financial literacy gives the organization the capability to make financially sound business decisions.

Building capability comes in a number of different forms. A very straightforward facet of capability is ensuring that our sales force has a granular understanding of the volume, mix, and pricing levers that drive our margins. On any given day, a salesperson has numerous choices when deciding how to pitch a customer on a variety of promotions among different products and packages. Each choice has an impact on the volume that will move through that account, as well as on the overall profitability for the customer and PBG.

Capability also comes in the form of tools. One tool we use is a very clear list of priorities for a particular selling period. The finance organization works with the leadership of our North American business to develop objectives that contribute to the company's operational and financial targets. While that might seem elementary at first blush, it is actually quite powerful when you can mobilize a sales force of more than 20,000 individuals across the United States to focus on the same, very specific selling objectives at the same time.

Capability also comes from what we call guardrails. The use of guardrails refers to specific parameters that should be used to evaluate the financial impact of various decisions. For example, we have hundreds of thousands of pieces of vending equipment, many of which operate on slim margins. Therefore, it is very important that our salespeople have clear criteria for the placement of this equipment to ensure that the company will receive a solid return on these assets.

Deliver Our Commitments

PBG is a very results-oriented company. We have a bias for action, and a passion for results. We set very high standards of performance for ourselves, and we hold each other accountable for delivering results. This tenet of our corporate culture cuts across all aspects of the company, including the finance organization.

At PBG, we understand that if a case of soda is not sold today, that opportunity is gone forever. We don't get a second chance to make that sale. Given the operational complexity and scope of our business, it is critically important that we drive deep into our culture the need to consistently deliver on our commitments day in and day out. That is true in our sales organization; it's true for the manufacturing and logistics operations, and equally true within our finance group.

More specifically in the finance organization, there are two types of commitments we need to deliver. The first is ensuring that the company delivers on the financial commitments we've made to our shareholders. This requires that we cascade those commitments down to the frontline of the organization at a very granular level. Every individual must understand the specific targets they must achieve day in and day out in order for the company to fulfill its promise in total. Once those targets are set and communicated effectively, we track progress against these goals in real time, providing insights for mid-course corrections.

The second type of commitment is one that the finance organization must deliver to the operating management of the company. When they look to us for insights and financial literacy, we must consistently fulfill those needs in a robust and timely fashion. This provides our management with the information and tools it needs to manage a highly transactional business.

Respect Each Other

In a dynamic environment like PBG, it is important that we have appropriate checks and balances to ensure that we achieve our results the right way.

We have a very diverse employee base that mirrors a very diverse set of customers and consumers. From kiosk owners in Russian markets to chain supermarkets in Michigan to mom and pop markets in rural Mexico, our customer base is very broad. In order to service these customers effectively, we need to have employees who can relate to and understand their unique needs. We strive to maintain a culture that embraces those differences and rewards results.

How to be a Successful CFO

There's a big premium these days on unyielding integrity. While this seems to be particularly topical these days, I have always believed integrity is the most important quality a chief financial officer should possess. Without it, a person cannot lead an organization. Ultimately, the absence of integrity will lead a company astray—as several recent and highly public examples have proven.

Another area that is very important for a CFO's success is breadth of experience. Clearly, there is a set of technical skills a CFO needs to possess. He or she needs to know how to perform financial analysis and understand the basics of accounting and planning, as well as the areas of treasury, tax, and regulatory requirements. But these are really just prerequisites for any leadership position in finance.

What sets apart an outstanding finance leader is someone who has broad business experience. This provides an individual with an instinctive understanding for what works in the operations and what is unlikely to work. I value more highly a financial executive who has a solid technical background and outstanding business sense, as opposed to someone who has a tremendous amount of technical experience, but little practical business acumen. Broad-based experience will help an individual tap into the pulse of what's going on within the company.

This type of breadth also improves a finance person's standing with the general management population. In order to have an impact with the operators of the company, we must be able to demonstrate that we understand the business and how it works. If they believe we're just technical experts, it's going to be very difficult to influence their plans and affect the business results. Without operating credibility, it can even be difficult to maintain effective controls.

An effective finance leader will have a seat at the table at all levels of the organization. His or her opinion should be sought out, and judgment should be trusted.

A successful CFO must also possess leadership qualities. There are several aspects of this leadership. As a CFO, a person must be able to lead the finance organization, but equally important is the ability to help shape a business agenda within the company.

The CFO role is unique in that the individual holding this title must not only be a leader of people internally, but he or she must also be able to communicate effectively with external audiences, from shareholders to financial analysts to regulatory agencies. This requires leadership with credibility.

Unique to the Industry

PBG is a consumer packaged goods company. The operationally intensive nature of our business, however, sets us apart from more traditional packaged goods companies. Our business is all about trucks going up and down the street with salespeople making hundreds of thousands of sales contacts every day.

In this environment, there is a premium placed on executional capability. Whether it's at the point of sale, on a line in one of our manufacturing plants, or in a training room at headquarters, executing the task at hand is critical to our success. It is no different for the finance organization. Our finance leaders must be able to lead large and diverse organizations. They must provide effective tools and business insights in real time. They must ensure a high level of integrity throughout the organization. And they must execute at a very high standard in real time.

Where We Look for Productivity

There are two major buckets of cost in our business. The first is the category of raw materials, and the second is labor. Raw materials comprise all of our product ingredients and packaging materials. Our labor costs are centered in our make, sell, deliver, and service activities.

The cost of raw materials has two primary components. The price of the underlying commodities is one. Examples include the price of the aluminum ingot that goes into our cans, the cost of resin that is used to produce plastic bottles, and the price of corn, which is a primary ingredient for some of our sweeteners. We are active in the commodity markets to limit the growth and volatility in the costs of these commodities.

We also look for ways to reduce our usage of these commodities. For example, we can accomplish this by reducing the amount of resin we use in our plastic bottles or even a bottle cap. We also try to reduce the amount of cardboard used in secondary packaging materials. The challenge in this area is to find ways to make these types of changes without compromising the high quality of our products and packaging.

In the area of labor, the primary way we can reduce costs is by increasing the productivity of our employees. For our sales force, we measure productivity in terms of the number of cases sold per employee. One example of a productivity initiative is a change in our selling and delivery system from conventional route delivery to a pre-sell system. The traditional selling and delivery method in the bottling industry has been the conventional route system. Under this format, a driver sold our products, delivered them to a store, and merchandised them on our customers' shelves. In pre-sell, we've segregated those activities so we have one person responsible for the selling and merchandising, and second individual that is responsible for the delivery of our products. This focus provides a heightened level of customer service, as well as greater productivity in each of these functions.

The second example of labor productivity improvements falls under the umbrella of technology. We have equipped our sales force with handheld computers that include a "smart selling" functionality. These handheld computers not only increased the effectiveness of our sales calls, but they also significantly reduce the amount of time our employees spend on administrative tasks.

In the finance organization, we look for ways to improve productivity as well. Our function used to be decentralized. In recent years, however, we have taken steps to centralize certain functions where appropriate. In doing so, we have left decision and business support resources in the operating units, but centralized transaction processing activities.

For example, last year we consolidated our payroll processing into our customer service center in North Carolina. Instead of having people in dozens of locations scattered across the United States processing payroll, we now have one core, highly specialized team in a single location. That move yielded three benefits. The first is that we now provide our 30,000-plus employees in the United States with better service in the area of payroll. Second, we have become far more efficient, which has translated into bottom line savings. And third, a streamlined and standardized payroll process has enhanced our internal control.

Opportunities for the Future

Communications technology is fertile ground for productivity initiatives. The nature of our business—with roughly 26,000 salespeople in the field every day—creates a variety of communication needs. While pagers are sufficient for certain jobs, others require cell phone access, and some need walkie-talkie technology. With more than 300 locations across the country and each office contracting with their own local supplier, we had ample opportunity to create efficiencies in this area.

Recently, we created national standards that addressed the specific mobile communication needs for each position in the field based on the requirements of the job. The next step was to negotiate a few select national contracts with equipment and service suppliers. These steps have generated significant cost savings for the company.

As technology progresses and new devices become available, we now have a formalized process for evaluating the benefit of making those available to our sales force.

Sarbanes-Oxley

Sarbanes-Oxley compliance work is enormously important. It's vital for the companies performing the work, and even more valuable for the shareholders who will gain increased confidence in the company as a result of the work.

Complying with this new law has been a work in progress. Regulations were released and clarified throughout the past year as companies were undertaking their compliance work. Even the largest accounting and audit firms were just finding their way through the first year. Because of this, there hasn't been an established set of best practices for companies to follow.

Most companies, PBG included, simply tried to share their knowledge and experiences, and draw upon those of other companies. We've done this informally by reaching out to other packaged goods companies. We've also pursued information in more formal settings, such as conferences conducted by the corporate executive board and other like organizations. Members of our audit committee have been very helpful by sharing their own insights and experiences from other companies with which they are associated.

The Financial Impact

Compliance with most new disclosure laws and regulations comes with a significant cost. In year one, we're investing about 40,000 man-hours to complete the Sarbanes-Oxley 404 Certification. The total cost will likely be in the range of $6 to $7 million.

As we look ahead to year two of compliance with this new legislation, we will be looking to build upon our learning and become more efficient. Many aspects of our compliance in year one will not need to be repeated entirely, so there will be some opportunity to bring those costs down in future years. For example, the documenting of all our control processes was a significant one-time expenditure. Looking ahead, we can simply update and refresh that portion of the certification.

Additionally, we expect to become more efficient in our testing processes. We also expect greater efficiencies from the work of our external auditors.

Becoming Prepared

At PBG, we reached out to numerous other companies across industries to learn how they were approaching this work. We then assembled an internal team to develop a plan to ensure that the company would be in full compliance with Sarbanes-Oxley. The work of this team was not focused solely on the internal control provisions of Sarbanes-Oxley, but also addressed topics such as risk management and evolving disclosure requirements.

Compliance with the regulations was a critical objective, but not our only one. We also wanted to ensure that we were providing an appropriate level of transparency in our business, as well as strengthening the controls.

An important first step in the plan was the creation of a disclosure committee. This committee is charged with rigorously reviewing virtually all information communicated externally. Whether it's a presentation at an investment conference, a 10K filing, or an earnings press release, this committee reviews the financials and the content of these communications to ensure that we are consistent and accurate.

The members of the disclosure committee include our:

- controller,
- treasurer,
- general counsel,
- vice president of investor relations,

- vice president of tax,
- director of financial reporting, and
- several other senior leaders from the finance organization.

The collective knowledge and expertise of this group has enabled us to substantially enhance the quality of our disclosure.

Last year, as we started this work, our controller was tasked with leading the company's Sarbanes-Oxley 404 certification work. We increased the staff of our internal audit group as they coordinated the detailed work of documentation and testing of our processes in operations around the world. Much of this work is being completed by the broader finance organization in partnership with our operating teams in the field.

As CFO, I have been actively involved with every aspect of this program from its inception. I believe it requires leadership and commitment from the top of the organization. The entire company recognizes the importance of this work and understands that our senior management is absolutely committed to meeting both the requirements and the spirit of these new laws.

Outside Groups

Given the fluid nature of these regulatory changes, it is important to gain the most up-to-date counsel on all aspects of compliance. At PBG, we relied heavily on our external auditors for guidance. We also sought outside legal counsel that specializes in regulatory compliance to help us understand our obligations. In this case, legal advice is almost as abundant and necessary as accounting advice.

For example, one component of the 404 certification of Sarbanes-Oxley is the identification of any control weaknesses. These weaknesses then need to be categorized into three distinct buckets:

1. First is "material weakness."
2. Second is "a significant deficiency."
3. Third is "inconsequential."

The category into which a weakness falls dictates the level of disclosure required. At the inconsequential end of the spectrum, a weakness can be dealt with internally and no further disclosure is required. A significant deficiency, however, must be discussed with the audit committee of a company's board of directors. And in the most extreme case of a material weakness, public disclosure is required.

At the start of this process, there was no guidance as to how to utilize these categories. During the course of the past year, a tremendous amount of discussion took place within the legal and accounting professions about the definitions of each of these categories and how potential weaknesses should be categorized.

Today, there are broad parameters for the categorization process, but no black-and-white definitions. As a result, judgment will continue to play an important role. This continues to be an area in which we seek as much outside advice as possible as we finalize our certification process.

Although we have used outside parties for advice, we ultimately are responsible for conducting this work properly, so we have relied heavily on internal resources and expertise to make final judgments. While some companies have elected to outsource much of the control documentation and testing that is required, we believe our intimate knowledge of our company's processes and the industry make us better suited to evaluate the information.

Summary

The role of a finance executive has grown more complicated, more demanding, and more important. The fiduciary and legal responsibilities of a CFO of a publicly traded company continue to increase, and I would expect that trend to continue. Our operating teams' needs for additional insights and support will continue to grow as well.

At PBG, I will continue to lead our organization under the mission of creating value for the company. We will focus on building the financial literacy of our operating organization, and assist them in identifying productivity initiatives. The key attributes the entire finance organization—

individually and collectively—must deliver to PBG are unyielding integrity, leadership, business breadth, and technical competence. Delivering on this commitment will generate greater shareholder value.

Alfred H. Drewes is senior vice president and chief financial officer of the Pepsi Bottling Group, Inc. (PBG). Elected to this position in June of 2001, Mr. Drewes previously served as senior vice president and chief financial officer of Pepsi-Cola International (PCI).

Mr. Drewes joined PBG in 1982 as a financial analyst in New Jersey. During the next nine years, he rose through increasingly responsible finance positions within Pepsi-Cola North America in field operations and headquarters. In 1991, Mr. Drewes joined PCI as vice president of manufacturing operations, with responsibility for the global concentrate supply organization. In 1994, he was appointed vice president of business planning and new business development and, in 1996, relocated to London as the vice president and chief financial officer of the Europe and sub-Saharan Africa business unit of PCI.

Mr. Drewes earned a bachelor's of science degree in electrical engineering from the University of Massachusetts in 1978, and an M.B.A. from Columbia University in 1982.

The Art of Being a CFO

Danyelle L. Kennedy-Lantz
Chief Financial Officer
Network Telephone

Money is the language of business, but knowing the words to a language does not make you an effective communicator. The art of being a CFO is recognizing how the operations of the business result in a financial impact. It is being able to utilize the past history of the company, along with an understanding of the economic and competitive environment, to project the future results. It is using that gut intuition of knowing the operations of a company, knowing what's happened in the past, and turning that into a crystal ball that can predict what's coming around the corner. To accomplish all this, of course, a CFO needs education, training, and experience. Yet the qualities that differentiate good CFOs are strong leadership abilities, the willingness to get involved in operations and understand them, strong communication skills, and a high level of integrity.

The challenge aspect of being a CFO is that there's so much change, from regulatory changes to competitive pressures, especially in our subset, the competitive local exchange carriers or CLECs of the industry. There's no putting a process in place and taking comfort in the fact that it's going to be the same in six months. As an example, the Triennial Review Order removed our access to TELRIC pricing. This resulted in a substantial increase in our cost of goods sold. Within forty-five days, we relaunched product sets and modified commissioning plans to respond to this regulatory change.

Another challenge is the misconception that the position is just a finance head. Some believe that CFOs don't necessarily understand the business, and that the "no's" that come out are often arbitrary or solely tied to numbers. Quite often, the individual contributor within an organization does not understand the role that finance performs within the business. I developed a training class that provides an overview of our business model, a brief history of the company, and the key performance metrics that management utilizes to measure success within the business. With an increased exposure has come a greater level of understanding of the corporate vision and the financial metrics that drive that vision. It has increased the support of the finance organization as well as encouraged quality decision making at the individual contributor level.

The role of the CFO has changed in the last few years. With Sarbanes-Oxley and all the scandals in the industry, CFOs are being held to a higher operational standard of knowledge of what's going on in the company. More and more, the roles of the CFO and CEO tend to blend in regard to what they're supposed to know and sign off on. Access to the CFO by the board of directors has been increasing in the amount and frequency of communication.

In the coming years, the same trends will probably continue. Now that the CFO is considered a more openly relied on source for understanding not only the financial, but also the operational, the standard of coming to the CFO to validate the operational performance and its impact on financials is going to continue.

The Scope of the CFO Position

The focus of the position of CFO is to ensure that the company grows profitably, to provide a return to the shareholders, and to create a positive and constructive environment for all of the stakeholders.

The position has a direct financial impact on the company through cash management, performance measurement and metrics, and risk management. Everything that happens within a company is either generating cash by generating revenue, or it is spending cash by creating an expense. From a cash management perspective, training classes on the business plan for all new employees help them understand what the business's drivers are, so that they're making good decisions on the front line. The focus must go from ensuring that the individual contributors in the business are making good business decisions all the way through typical treasury management functions—how the cash is spent, making sure there's a return on investment for any capital items, and pulling back on expenses if the organization is not on track with any revenue targets.

The resources most useful to the CFO position are the people. Shareholder groups can be utilized for ideas, experience, and comparative analysis to peers within the industry that they have. Employees have resources and experiences from a variety of backgrounds as well as firsthand knowledge of the customer's experience with the organization. Rarely is something done in a company that is happening for the first time in the world. Other people have faced similar problems, and much can be learned from how they tackled them, or where they have had other success. Companies can utilize those similar principles to obtain that same success in their market. Our company is more people-oriented as our primary resource, rather than looking at trade magazines or external research tools.

One of the more difficult situations someone in the position faces is recognizing when cost reductions must be made and reaching the conclusion that the largest controllable expense within the organization is headcount. Layoffs never get easier, and if they ever do, that's when it's time to get out of the job. From the initial challenge of running various business model scenarios to project what the optimum headcount is for the company to reach its operational objectives and to minimize costs, to remembering that those ones and twos on the spreadsheet are actually people, and that this decision is affecting their lives, that's when it hits home.

As with any crisis, communicating the reasons for the change and how the decisions are reached is necessary to obtain the buy-in and support of the organization. It is critical that the CFOs take the time to lead the management team through the decision making process and the various business model scenarios so that each level of management understands the decisions being implemented and can garner the support of the employee base. Managing the strategic path decisions and guiding the management team to decisions that are fair and equitable to the employees affected while obtaining the cost savings that are needed is never simple. How this process is handled directly correlates to whether there is any employee-related litigation, unplanned attrition due to concern surrounding the layoff, and the overall morale of the employee base.

Active operational involvement and detailed-level business planning are good executive strategies for managing rapid company growth and ensuring increased profits. In the active operational involvement perspective, the CFO participates in the operational staff meetings alongside the COO, keeps abreast of priorities and challenges at a detailed level with the engineering and IT organizations, and reviews and questions detailed weekly reports from operations, which include everything from how quickly customer service personnel are answering the phone to how quickly trouble tickets are being resolved. The investment of being in those meetings and being able to speak to the individual contributors about their jobs allows the open communication that is critical for the CFO to understand not only what's going on in the business, but how it can be improved.

In order to achieve a high-quality detailed-level business plan, our company completes a "bottoms-up" budgeting process. The only information given to managers in each department is a blank template with the sales targets forecasted by month for the next two years. Outside of that, the template is completely blank so that each manager must decide how many people they need, how much and what type of capital expenditures they need, and what objectives or processes changes they need to support the sales forecast for their department. Their department is their own company. The managers form the overall business strategy of the company so they can make their departments as profitable as they can be. Each time the managers get better at the process, and they understand the drivers of the business and where they as individual managers can contribute to the overall success of the company.

Working with Others

The CFO works most closely with the CEO and COO. Second to that would be the head of sales and head of engineering. To get a great team established, it takes time to build a relationship, know the others' strengths and weaknesses, and recognize how each can support the others. CFOs have to know what each of the executives' priorities are so that the CFO can try to help the others succeed in their positions, since the cash management is typically all in the CFO's bucket. The other thing CFOs must know is where the risks are in each of the organization's departments. For example, if the Sales Department tells the CFO they're going to hit a certain sales number, what are the top ten things that could happen that could cause them to miss that target, and then what can be done to mitigate those risks to ensure the company hits its established goals. Defining what level of miss, although negative, does not impair the organization's ability to achieve.

With rapid growth and complex changes, the skills sets of the executive team members are critical. At the executive level, personality profiling is often done to ensure there's a good cultural fit and that everyone has the same goals in mind for how the business should be run. The culture of the company is set by all of the leaders in the company, not just the CEO. A focused effort must be made to see that the people brought into the company management have open communication styles. Consensus building skills are important, but being able to make a decision and execute in line with the corporate vision is even more so. Positive attitudes and high energy levels are important, especially in demanding industries such as telecom.

We have found the best way to set goals for the team is to bring the management team together to establish the corporate objectives. At the beginning of each year, the CFO team goes through a process of evaluating what their strategic objectives for the upcoming year are. Part of that is the bottoms-up budgeting process, but the other piece is looking at it with a "the world is your oyster" type of perspective and imagining what could be accomplished; if you ignore how little cash or how much debt you have, imagine what you could make happen with the business and customer base you have. Once they brainstorm with a "the sky's the limit" approach, they narrow it down to the goals they can most likely achieve and have the best return with. Then they work to put them in place.

The goals are set on both an annual as well as a quarterly basis for the individual level, the departmental level, as well as the company as whole. To manage this effectively, a dashboard system has been developed known as the "Key Performance Indicators" or "KPIs." KPIs are a list of about the top fifteen to twenty financial metrics that are truly critical for measuring the success of the company. Although financial metrics such as day's sales outstanding and average revenue per line are important, it is the operational metrics that give you advanced insight into the future financial performance of the company. This allows you to quickly identify if the wheels are falling off the wagon, or if the wagon's running off the road. KPIs are tracked at the individual department level, where applicable, so that comparisons can be done on a daily and weekly basis to determine if each department is reaching its goals. For example, if you set a sales goal of five thousand lines sold by the end of the month, you know you're going to have to have so many full quota bearing sales representatives to sell an established average amount per business day to achieve that goal. If you can see that you do not have the expected number of headcount or that the average daily performance is below expectations, it provides advanced visibility into missing the monthly sales target. This allows the CFO to brief key members of management as well as the board of directors, when needed, to ensure that no one is caught off guard.

To ensure not only the success of the company, but to ensure its longevity, it is important that the difference between mission critical performance levels and goals is established and known. The mission critical level of performance would dictate the minimum expected performance that the company has to achieve to maintain expected cash flow levels. The next level, which ideally should be established within the budget process, defines what each department believes that they can accomplish and defines the base level of the bonus targets of the organization. This is what the company commits as expectations to the board of directors, and since they are achievable goals, the team knows it can meet them. When they hit the business plan, it's a great day, but they also know they haven't done everything they can do. The next level of achievement is when they hit their bonus targets, because that's when they are performing consistently above the business plan. Those achievements indicate true success.

Telecom as a Model

Some work of a CFO can be unique to the industry. For example, in the telecom industry, the unique skill set in the last few years has been crisis management, which highlights the need for strong leadership and communication skills. The telecom industry overall, as well as the CLEC industry specifically, has been on the decline for the past five years. Financing and equity alternatives have been limited. Maximizing what assets the company has and getting a return on those assets is the only option available. With the overhang of the MCI/WorldCom scandal, as well as the billions lost in telecommunications investments since the Internet bubble burst, integrity within the finance organization is critical.

In the telecom industry, the CFO and his/her team are a support organization. Finance's role from a general ledger perspective is to provide timely, meaningful, financial information to help the company management team make good business decisions. Some CFOs have purchasing and warehouse within their specific divisions. From that organization, they help drive purchasing decisions to be cost effective, to meet managers' and customers' needs, and to ship products out in a timely fashion—ideally before the customers ever know they need it. Some finance departments also oversee the collections group, which focuses on helping drive the cash collections of the company. The motto in collections should be "the buck stops here." If any other group in the company has failed to address a customer's need, and that's why the customer is keeping their money hostage. The collections group makes sure the customer's issue is resolved so that company can receive payment. Another group that can report directly to the CFO is facilities management, which handles both leasing strategies for locations as well as supporting those locations from a housekeeping perspective. The focus is on providing a safe and secure environment.

The CFO team has three categories of large expenses. The first category is capital expenditures. This includes small dollar, high volume items, such as customer premise equipment (CPE), that are required to install customers to larger high dollar, low volume items such as upgrading software and hardware equipment. The second driver and largest expense to our organization is employee salaries and related benefits. Where the team chooses to add a person in the company is a critical decision that gets a lot of debate. If only ten people can be added a year, the team is forced to focus on which ten people to add and which positions are really going to give the most return. The third expense is the cost to goods sold, which includes the fixed costs of operating our telecommunications network, including connectivity, utilities and rent expense, and any fees paid to provide ancillary services to our customers through partnering/wholesale relationships. Managing vendor relationships to minimize costs and ensure quality is essential to maximizing profitability, as well as understanding that the regulations that drive those costs are sometimes out of the company's control. Outside of these three main expense categories, everything else is relatively small. Watching for trends and changes as a percentage of revenue ensures that these expenses stay in line with the growth of the organization.

With research and development, new ideas come from all across the company. In providing the vision of the company, as well as an understanding of the economic, competitive, and financial drivers of the company, employees are the source for the best suggestions. Employee suggestions can be submitted anonymously or with their name, to a suggestion box. Additionally, the executive team actively reads numerous trade magazines, staying on top of new technology and new trends that are emerging. Team members also talk to the sales force to see what the customers want—what services they are asking for that aren't currently provided. Once an idea is developed, the team members pull together assumptions on what they think it's going to cost and what it's going to be able to sell for, and they do a business plan. If that makes sense, they move forward to test the product out and try to break it to see where the flaws of the technology are. Then they move from an engineering technology to a market trial to see if it will sell the way they want it to sell. Then they validate all the assumptions on a more detailed function plan, go to the board for approval, and then they launch.

A CFO's Golden Rules

Confess before you get caught. If you know you have a negative trend within the operations or financial side of the business, even before it creates a defined and measurable financial impact, be up front and make sure your management team and board of directors is aware of the risk—try not to ever catch anyone off guard.

Always be honest. If you lose your credibility, whether dealing with customers, your employees, or your vendors, you really can't get it back. This is especially critical in managing a crisis, as the temptation so often is to say nothing until you have determined the solution to the problem. The reality is that the tension is always noticeable and most people's imaginations come up with far worse scenarios than the reality of the problem being faced. Stepping forward and stating the issue and your understanding of the potential range of affects, from good to bad, alleviates the stress of the unknown. People are extremely resilient and will always give you the benefit of the doubt if you are honest with them.

Take a deep breath, ask questions, don't assume anything, and escalate. So often when faced with a challenge, individuals rush to find a solution before taking the time to evaluate the problem. The result is solving a symptom, but not the root cause of the problem.

Danyelle L. Kennedy-Lantz joined Network Telephone in March 1999 as controller. She was promoted to vice president of finance a year later, then to senior vice president of finance in 2001. Serving as chief financial officer since May 2002, she is responsible for all financial aspects of the company, including financial operations, business forecasting and budgeting, banking, risk management, financial reporting, merger and acquisition activity, collections and purchasing, and warehouse management.

From 1993 to 1999, Ms. Lantz was an audit senior at Arthur Anderson, LLP, where she specialized in telecommunications and banking. Her clients included several publicly traded companies, including a multi-national wireless telecommunications company with assets of $740 million, a long distance telephone company with $50 million in assets, a commercial bank with more than $2.5 billion in assets, and a state public employee retirement system with assets of $14 billion.

Lantz graduated magna cum laude from the University of Southern Mississippi with an accounting degree, and earned her CPA (Certified Public Accountant) for the state of Mississippi. She lives with her husband, Tyler, in Pensacola, Florida.

Dedication: *Dedicated to my loving husband, Tyler.*

Real-Life CFO Management

Sam B. Bruce

Executive Vice President and Chief Financial Officer

Star Software Systems Corporation

Responsibilities of a CFO

Simply put, a CFO chases money. People often perceive this as the only role of a CFO; however, he or she is also a member of the strategic team that directs the company for success. The job of a CFO entails monitoring and providing money for all the operational and strategic objectives of a company. In any company, executives should review the strategic plan for an upcoming year and lay out specific goals that are aligned with the overall objectives of a company. After determining goals for the upcoming year, they should consider goals and strategies beyond the next year. These goals then become the basis for the vision of the company and are written on a Vision-Philosophy-Principle-Mission sheet. This document is the "shining light" for the company and lists the basic concepts under which the company operates. In technology, these visions frequently involve providing superior technology-based solutions for increasing an organization's efficiency, productivity, and profit while maintaining a reputation for excellence, integrity, and professionalism.

From a CFO's perspective, the important component of this vision is the word "profit." The goal of a CFO is ensuring that a profit is made while the company pursues the overall vision and principles of the company. Profitability must be integrated into all the objectives of a company. In addition to broad objectives, a CFO must ensure that the company meets its short-term, tactical objectives in a profitable manner throughout the year.

The Impact of a CFO

Within a company, a CFO ensures that money exists for the owners, the directors, and the shareholders. As a senior executive, I reviewed over 1400 businesses and their practices. In businesses with revenues of less than $15 million, most of the money was spent paying bills first. As a result, little or no money was left for the owners. One successful option is for a CFO to instigate "Sam's 8 percent rule," in which eight cents of every dollar goes into a savings account and 92 cents goes into an operating account. In essence, a company pays the stockholders first from the savings account while paying expenses from the operating account. At the end of the year, the savings account can be used to give bonuses to employees, buy capital equipment, and return hard dollars to the stockholders—even if there is only one stockholder.

The second impact of a CFO is monitoring billable hours. Administrative salaries in general are overhead; however, work for a client is billable hours. When a CFO gives a particular client a bill for an individual's service and that client pays, those billable hours pay that salary. If someone is billable but is not able to be on an invoice to send to a client, they therefore are non-billable. A CFO must explain to the executives and senior leadership that if somebody is not billable, the money does not come out of overhead, but directly out of profit. It is important that employees understand this concept because individuals that are non-billable cut into employee rewards at the end of the year.

A third way in which CFO affects a company is by telling the company story. He or she helps compile press releases and campaign packets. Often these releases detail the successes and rewards of the company. This was the key to winning "Small Business Person of the Year" for the state of Georgia in 2005.

Successful Strategies and Characteristics of a CFO

In order to foster leadership within a company's workforce, the executive board should choose two or three individuals who consistently deliver value, work hard, and accomplish tasks successfully to have leadership access. These individuals should be taught/learn the overall direction of the company, the location of resources within the company, and projects that are generally not known. By expanding their knowledge in such a way, a company can identify future leaders and keep information flowing to them. The company should envision these individuals as running a division of the company in the future. Through this indirect line of communication, this group is able to maintain moral, help clients, and reduce rumor and friction because they can speak to their peer group from a knowledge base. This allows them to do things others would not be able to do as a result of having the information.

Another successful strategy is making a company lean, or better, stronger, and faster. A company should constantly be evaluating its business with this lean-enterprise approach. As a result, a company should pursue value stream mapping throughout its infrastructure and that of its client. Value stream mapping is one part of the LEAN process that looks at processes from start to finish. The data gained from this mapping can then be used to analyze how a company can improve on specific projects. This provides the basis for positive change.

For a CFO to be successful, he or she must learn the art of telling the story of a company so that investors and employees want to invest their capital. For employees, this investment is not monetary but personal. For example, an employee takes tasks they do not want to do because it is best for the team. In order to tell the story of the company to an investor, a CFO must describe the direction of the company by answering questions about the future of the company before they ask.

Overall, the best advice for a CFO is to use all the resources and energy necessary to finish a task that must be accomplished. He or she should use the resources necessary, but avoid wasting time and money. Serving as a task force leader, subject matter expert, or giving directions at senior staff meetings focuses resources.

Working with Other Executives

A chief financial officer works closely with the president in order to do what is right for the customers of a business. Frequently, these individuals think alike; therefore, they agree on the same course of action. Once the vision and mission of the company are established and agreed to by the senior staff, a basis for a good working relationship exists. Both the CEO and the CFO must agree to disagree on business issues and even get passionate about specific items. However, it cannot get personal or be taken personally, or the relationship is on the way to ending. If the relationship turns to "not working in cooperation with each other," two things should happen. The CFO should detail in writing to the CEO what he perceives the problem and solution to be and the CFO must be prepared to go to the board, or resign if the problem is not resolved.

Team Members

When looking for a team member, a CFO wants an individual who is capable of saying "No." As a result, he or she finds individuals who have the fortitude to identify ineffective tasks or strategies and bring them to the surface of the process. An individual must be able to have responsibility, accountability, and trust. The main quality required of a team member, however, is hard work: an individual with an average education who works hard is still a hard worker. A highly educated individual, who is lazy, unfortunately is still lazy.

The goals of team members are based on the goals of the company. Once the goals are set, the team members should be monitored through peer reviews and supervisory reviews. They should be evaluated technically as well as managerially. This combination of reviews then becomes the basis for retaining employment, future training and education, and future bonuses. As a result, team members are self-motivated and are expected to have a passion for excellence, a dedication to the company, as well as accountability and responsibility.

Overcoming Challenges

The main challenge of a CFO is following cash flow. By using offsite meetings and tactical and strategic objective lists, a CFO and his team can maintain a focus on the cash flow. In order to follow it, however, they must understand where the cash flow is going and if it is effective and profitable in that area. When projects are completed, the specific jobs associated with them also conclude. As a result, a company must move cash flow either to another project by finding another specific job for an individual or must end the cash flow drain by laying them off.

Another challenge is to make sure audits of the company are completed. In companies that handle government contracts, a federal agency called the Defense Contract Audit Agency (DCAA) can audit these companies at any time. As a result, companies must complete tasks on time on a daily basis. In order to facilitate the timely completion of tasks, a technology company should consider moving to a precise software package that is compliant and accepted by the DCAA. Close attention should also be given to following stringent accounting rules and principles.

Expenses

The largest expense of a technology company is development. With the advent of government contracting, teaming with similarly sized and larger companies has increased. This group then submits a proposal to win a bid; this process can take as long as a year. This form of development is a significant risk because the group is not guaranteed the contract. Commercially, software development creates large costs because frequently the individuals who develop software are non-billable. As a result, a company must be careful about the projects it chooses to develop. A one million dollar mistake will kill a small company, where it is just a mistake in a multi-billion dollar company.

Two distinct challenges arise during development: acquiring new work and selling a new product. Each requires money that possibly does not create money in return. As a result, a company should carefully discuss these issues in strategic management planning groups and then make allocations for each of these development areas.

Technology itself can also be expensive. From the financial perspective, technology creates challenges because the price of technology is constantly changing. When new technology comes to the market, it is expensive but gradually decreases as time passes. The obvious comparison is the personal computer. When it was introduced, a typical model would cost up to $5,000. Today a far more powerful machine costs less than $400. Then, as today, cost benefit to the bottom line is the deciding factor in making the investment.

Research and Development

In order to encourage research and development despite these costs, a company should consider applying for a small business innovative research grant (SBIR) from the National Science Foundation or other government research department. These grants serve as predictive analysis tools and generally have different phases of development. For example, the National

Science Foundation offers a research grant divided into three phases. Phase one involves an initial money grant. In phase two, more money is given to the company to develop the commercialized product. Phase three is taking the product to market without additional grant money. This process allows a company to discover a product that could only be researched at a larger company, as well as to validate the benefits of the product.

The Changing Role of the CFO

Recent media coverage of the CFOs that have committed crimes blames the companies that betrayed the trust of the stockholders. This exposure spreads a general lack of awareness as to the role of the CFO within the company. In small companies prior to an IPO, the few stockholders know the CFO well. In larger companies, the CFO and auditors must now act together to be the "checks and balances" for best business practices to regain any trust lost during recent coverage.

The position will also change with the legal ramifications in regards to Sarbanes-Oxley. The simple tool the legislation provided is a lever to get things done by the CFO based in law.

Technology has and will continue to change the role of the CFO because financial data can be queried by software and answers to hard questions are available now. There is not the long wait for the audit that could take weeks or months. Therefore the CFO must be experienced and educated enough to take the emerging data and then almost instantly explain the impact these results would have for the company and for a client.

In conclusion, it is critical to understand that the CFO and CEO must be a team that works toward the success of the company. The CFO must be a positive force that provides sage advice based in fact, that is founded in the belief that we are in business to make a profit.

Sam B. Bruce holds a master's degree from the University of South Carolina and received his B.S. with honors from the University of Southern Mississippi. He serves as executive vice president for Corporate Affairs and CFO of STAR. He served as a senior executive and senior business analyst for seven years with a large consulting firm in Chicago before working full time at STAR. He also served as chief of staff for the SC Department of Education. He served as a part-time consultant to STAR for ten years.

Mr. Bruce served as a military officer who was involved extensively in the design, development, implementation, and support of management information systems, business solutions, and instructional technology for government and commercial clients for more than twenty years. His wealth of experience in management, product development, and consulting at senior level positions includes the position of Director of Information Management (DOIM) at a major U.S. military installation, and management/operations positions in Europe, the Far East, and Washington D.C. His responsibilities included all five disciplines in Information Resource Management (IRM). Mr. Bruce is a graduate of the Armed Forces Staff College, PME, EEI courses, and senior IBM schools.

Balancing Short-Term and Long-Term Solutions in the Manufacturing Industry

Mary Valenta

Chief Financial Officer

O'Neal Steel, Inc.

Manufacturing will continue to thrive in the United States despite the exodus to countries with lower labor costs. The demand for continually increasing productivity, however, must endure. Companies may further dissect each operating function in the quest for continuous improvement.

Companies with proprietary products will continue to focus their business on research and development, sales, and marketing functions, while outsourcing their manufacturing to companies that are experts at operations. This simplifies the focus for each business, allowing each company to do what they do best. A contract manufacturer can better capitalize square footage and equipment, and employ direct labor by managing several projects and limiting risk of a shut down if any one project declines. Because quality controls are crucial to the end product, proprietary companies might still maintain the final assembly functions after contract manufacturers have completed the parts and sub-assemblies. Using operational experts will not only reduce costs, but will also increase the speed and quality of production.

Manufacturing is a much more detailed industry than most service sectors. Generally, manufacturing companies are capital intense and must manage myriad factors within the pricing, purchasing, operations, and cost accounting areas. A great understanding of the operations, research of each activity, and a complex analysis is usually required in setting appropriate standard key performance indices and costs. Measuring, reporting, and taking action on variances is critical. The trick then is to keep the measurements as simple as possible. To succeed, manufacturing companies need to keep their focus on a few key issues at once until those can be mastered, then continue to improve in other areas.

As a privately held, family-owned company, O'Neal Steel can make decisions that are best in the long term for customers, employees, and shareholders. Publicly owned companies are under constant pressure from shareholders and analysts to produce short-term results that may not be in the customer's or the company's best interests long term. O'Neal is also large enough to make quick decisions, without being overly bureaucratic.

Additionally, O'Neal's staff works closely with its customers to assist them in best practices throughout their operations. Our operational experts work with customers in the engineering of products to ensure the appropriate materials are being used. We have processing engineers that understand the product's use and requirements, review the specs, and offer alternatives based on their extensive knowledge of the metallurgic content, treatments, and capabilities of various metal products. Our plant employees who are experienced with lean manufacturing, 5-S, and six sigma programs will review a customer's operational setup, product flow and distribution methods, offering suggestions on continuous improvements. Additionally, our sales staff works closely with customers to assist in developing a realistic and viable forecast that assists the customer and us in the planning process.

My three golden rules for success are:

1. Keep an eye on the big picture while managing the details. Most managers are either visionaries or into the details. It's critical for a manager to assess what he or she is weaker at and practice it to improve the balance with his or her strengths. For example, I used to be a very detailed, hands-on manager. I had to force myself to delegate the details to other employees and step back to assess the big picture to ensure the overall goal was met most effectively.

2. Manage for the long-term term while achieving most of the short-term objectives. Often decisions are made quickly during a crisis mode or with a crunch deadline. However, in the long-run it is beneficial to take some extra time to assess the long-term impact of solutions so that others are not burdened with improper results in the future.

3. Treat employees well so they will in turn take good care of customers. So many companies state that customers are their number one priority, but then neglect or mistreat employees to the extent that employees are demoralized in dealing with customers. The end result is that customers really aren't getting the best service. Customer service is the most critical area to provide employee empowerment. Empowered employees have higher self-esteem and greater job satisfaction. Their enthusiasm reaches the customer, who in turn prefers to do business with that company.

Generating Growing Revenues and Profits

O'Neal expands its revenue base by identifying sales and economic trends in the various industries we serve, by determining customers' needs and expanding our capabilities to fit those needs, and by expanding industry expertise to further penetrate our market share. Because we have numerous operating locations, we can select the best fit for a specific project based on required equipment, labor content, and current available capacity. Start-up costs can be significant on a project, so it is important that a customer's order is large enough for us to absorb these initial costs.

Successful products are those with long-term growth opportunities that provide a higher return than other products and that have a fairly constant demand. Factors to determine profitability include carrying charges on inventory levels and accounts receivable balances, which make lead times on supply and industry payment terms critical. We also include all indirect costs such as sales and administration and corporate allocations.

The Challenges

A challenging part of the business is the volatility of customer orders. Forecasting demand is difficult when so much is driven by economic currents. The ebbs and flows require constant monitoring of direct labor use and subjectivity in the efficiency models. When labor is slow, we have to weigh the risk of layoffs with the significant cost of rehiring and training.

Contract manufacturers rely on their customers for forecasting production volumes. To succeed, manufacturers must stay close to the customers and their associations. Trends need to be monitored closely and acted on immediately.

The Competition

Our competitive advantage lies in making it simple for customers to do business with us, and ensuring we provide on-time delivery in any unexpected circumstances. O'Neal excels at assisting customers when they need flexibility because we are large enough to provide solutions to exceptional issues and yet small enough to be flexible and make quick decisions for customers at the direct level needed. ' The passion and drive from the O'Neal family creates an environment between suppliers, employees, and customers that stimulates sales growth. Customers are impressed with the owners' involvement and commitment to meeting their needs.

The Expenses

The raw material cost of steel, especially during the extraordinary price run up over the past year and a half, continues to be our largest cost. The volatility in this market wreaks havoc on contract pricing with mills and with customers. Surcharges due to scrap prices have added to this dilemma. Current attempts to create a futures exchange in steel commodities will eventually lead to more stable pricing.

Freight and fuel costs have also become a significant issue in cost and in availability. Availability of flatbed common carrier trucks has been limited due to a low supply/high demand mode. Also, rising medical costs have plagued our industry, as they have others.

Ensuring and Measuring Success

To keep our edge with respect to our customer base, we are involved in many of our customers' industry associations, as well as in our own industry association. The National Association of Manufacturers sponsors many excellent publications and events that address particular issues.

We continuously meet with key customers to keep abreast of their changes and needs. Our senior management, including our company owners, strategically evaluates each key account for service levels, value-added opportunities, and growth potential at least quarterly. As CFO, I spend a good deal of time with customers learning how we can meet their specific needs and help each other grow sales.

We also hold periodic executive strategy updates and involve as many employees as possible in each strategic initiative. Each district is responsible for periodic sales and operational reports. Most importantly, non-exempt salaried staff's compensation is tied to performance results measured by economic value added. Each district is charged for its level of inventory and accounts receivable, as well as a fixed rate for real property and capital equipment. Incentives are tied to the extent operating profits exceed these charges. This gives each district the authority to do whatever necessary to maintain efficient levels of assets and to maximize capacity.

To measure success, we establish corporate goals and consequent district/department goals so that all employees are working toward the same results. Our strategic team involves a cross-functional management group who focus on sales growth, operational efficiency, and employee satisfaction goals. On a corporate basis, we measure economic value added returns by district; basically, adding carrying charges for inventory, accounts receivable, and capital expenditures to earnings before interest, taxes, depreciation, and amortization expense. Additionally, my team has individual quarterly goals that include personal development. A key component of the company's culture is employee satisfaction. Our strategic focus for employees is on recruiting, development, retention, and reward systems.

Changes in the Industry

Over the last ten to fifteen years, the industry has seen a mass exodus to lower wage countries, as well as growth in outsourcing manufacturing. Another development over the years has been the use of six-sigma programs. Electronic transactions and higher-tech equipment, such as robotics, have also changed the industry.

Not all developments are so positive. Our labor force is becoming more and more limited due to lower math and verbal competence and pervasive drug use. The number of candidates who do not know basic math, such as the number of inches in a foot, is disappointing. Even more disturbing is how many candidates do not pass our mandatory drug test. We have found our most successful recruiting efforts are from employee referrals. Additionally, we have broadened our searches through Internet job sites. Hopefully, the political focus on "no child left behind" will improve the future of the American workforce.

Over the next five to ten years, advances in technology and operational focus will further improve productivity. Enterprise resource planning applications for manufacturing must be made more flexible and yet be less complex to run. So many manufacturing companies are bogged down with implementing or maintaining information technology systems that provide insufficient value for the effort expended.

Businesses will continue to assess their core competencies and restructure to specialize by function, not just within an industry or a product group. Some companies will enhance product development by focusing efforts and funding on innovation, R&D projects, and marketing/sales. These companies will outsource their operations functions to companies that have the fixed assets and expertise in manufacturing. The effect of focused specialization for both companies will be improved efficiencies and lowered costs.

The Role of the CFO

CFOs face a number of challenges unique to their position because they are required to balance many things. First, CFOs must balance the big picture with the details. CFOs must be hands on enough to understand some complex and technical issues, but then stay at the 30,000-foot level to assess the company's vision and direction.

CFOs also have to balance the short term with the long term. CFOs must, for example, make fairly quick decisions based on knowing the details and the broad issues and balance short-term and long-term solutions. Shareholders and analysts may pressure for short-term solutions that may compromise long-term results for the company. For example, an underperforming unit may be closed almost immediately to reduce short-term costs; however, in the long term that unit may have the opportunity to turn around and provide net profit to the company. Weighing short-term and long-term effects requires constant alternative/risk analysis, experience, and good judgment.

Sales growth versus operation issues represents another area that CFOs must balance. CFOs are challenged with assisting non-finance managers, such as sales, marketing, and operations, from a business and financial perspective. Some issues, such as credit decisions, require balancing desired sales growth with safe collections of receivables. CFOs often lead cost cutting measures, but doing so without investigation and insight may actual hinder sales. For example, cutting certain skilled labor may result in quality issues, and eventually, lost sales.

To face each of these challenges, set objectives and expectations at high levels right from the beginning, always consider the long-term impact on the business, and work closely with functional heads, keeping all apprised of decisions and results.

Over the next six months, CFOs will continue to face unique challenges, including those formed by the American Jobs Creation Act of 2004, in determining manufacturing tax credits and in managing changes to non-qualified deferred compensation plans. The implementation of Sarbanes-Oxley for privately held companies may be required by lending institutions or Board of Directors. These companies will need to review and document stronger internal controls. CFOs will need to manage the changes in cash flow as a result of the Check 21 Act. These are interesting challenges that will require research and analysis by CFOs, and should provide great opportunities to strengthen and improve company policies and procedures.

To conquer the American Jobs Creation Act, we will consult with our tax partner on analyzing our manufacturing processes and develop a template to measure qualified expenses. We have already identified and implemented changes to our non-qualified deferred compensation plan with the help of an outside expert.

For Sarbanes-Oxley, we will make recommendations to our Board on feasible solutions for critical issues and implement them in prioritized order. Our initial focus is on creating an Audit Charter and an Audit Committee, strengthening our documentation of internal controls, and obtaining departmental certifications.

The Check 21 Act will lead us to consult with banking and technical firms on taking advantage of Check 21 to provide solutions to long-term issues, such as COD and remote deposits.